Confessions of a Wedding Planner

A Guide to Talking the 'Zilla' Out of the Bride

Bessy Vazzocchi

Confessions of a Wedding Planner

ISBN: 1500501484
ISBN-13: 978-1500501488

Cover design by Bessy Vazzocchi

Dedicated to the little peanut growing inside me.

Contents

Acknowledgements

Thank you to my parents for raising me to be half literate and teaching me that I can do whatever I want. Thank you to my dear friends Tanya and Adriana for helping me with the editing in the very beginning stages of this book when I had no idea what I was doing. Thank you to my sister Julie for being brutally honest with me with certain parts of this book that have been removed because, simply, they sucked. Thank you to my husband Mark for all his quirky opinions with the content and cover design from day one to the day we went to print. Most importantly, thank you to my friends, my family and my clients for allowing me to be a part of their special days. Without the erratic, irrational behavior of my brides when planning their weddings, I wouldn't have such hilarious stories to tell that future brides can learn from. Thank you to my sister in law Lisa who allowed me to over exaggerate her tiny wedding glitches into complete disaster stories for comedic effect. Without you all, none of this would be possible. Thank you to my readers and followers on Facebook, Instagram and Twitter.

From the bottom of my heart to you all, thank you.

Author's Note

Names have been changed. Characters and events have been combined, compressed and reordered. Stories have been exaggerated.

Preface

Here's what I'm not. I'm not one of the country's top 10 wedding planners. I don't have a crazy advertizing budget that will allow me to feature my company on luxe wedding sites and blogs. I'm not a celebrity wedding planner who will make all your wedding dreams come true with the wave of my magic wand. I'm not connected to all the top wedding vendors in the country who also have crazy advertizing budgets and I'm certainly not famous. What I am, is a passionate, OPPINIONATED wedding planner who thinks the wedding world is full of very well marketed bullshit. I'm a lover of weddings who simply believes they've derailed and have lost their true meaning which is a celebration of two individuals starting the rest of their lives together. I am committed to providing awesome services to my clients so they can tell their friends and family about me. That's how I advertize. I'm connected to under the radar vendors who are just as awesome and passionate about what they do as I am and who will help make your day nothing short of perfect. I'm a little fish in a very big pond. I'm not going to change the world with this book. I just have something to say and I'm grateful for you, the reader, who is willing to listen.

1

So You're Getting Married...

You're engaged. Congratulations!!! Now, DO NOT freak out. If you've picked up this book then chances are you're a sensible, grounded person who is not an ego-maniac. You're super busy and you don't have all the time in the world to plan the wedding of the century. Seriously, you don't have time. He's popped the question and those "I Do's" are months, if not weeks away. Because who wants to be engaged for half a decade? If you're in the long engagement boat, this book may not be for you. If you're still interested, I suggest you keep a very open mind and you may even find yourself walking down the aisle a lot sooner than later. You're more concerned about day two of your marriage, followed by the rest of your life rather than the first eight hours of day one.

Far too many people spend twelve to thirty-six

months obsessing over this one day. This one very expensive, and not to mention, exhausting day. I'm here to tell you a few things. Sorry to be the bearer of bad news, but for one, no one is refreshing their newsfeed waiting for every intricate wedding detail of yours. Secondly, other peoples' lives do still go on during your extended engagement. Your friends and family don't all live in a world where baby's breath and votive candles are hot conversation topics. Change the channel from the Me Show and realize you and your wedding are not the only things that exist for the duration of your engagement.

Oh, and one more thing to help with your reality check: When the clock strikes midnight it's time to take off the $10,000 Lazaro dress and hang up your Jimmy Choos, put them in a box you're never going to open again and finally go to the bathroom. Your big day is over because guess what ladies? Even Cinderella's fairy godmother couldn't make time stand still. Time doesn't stop for anyone so in no time you'll be at someone else's wedding. That "someone else" watched you very closely while you were planning. She was probably the only one who gave a shit when you talked about all your creative, never done before ideas that you thought would go down in wedding history. Why, you ask? So she can one up you. Before you know it, you're sitting at her wedding critiquing every little detail while yours is a distant memory. Sadly, unless you're a Kardashian, you don't have an unlimited budget or an unlimited number of dream weddings (in Kim's case) and you don't have the luxury of paying your big day off with one cheque you earned just for flashing your ass in Paper Magazine. And seriously, who cares? You're doing it all for who? That girl who is taking notes at your wedding so she can make hers better? Then when she succeeds you're left with a hefty bill and a new "frenemy". If these things are your main focus then maybe you should circle back to the question of why you're getting married in the first place. Is it to impress your peers and frenemies or is it because you want to start the next chapter of your life with the one you love? If it's the latter then all that competition nonsense should not matter.

If you're willing to wake up from your fairytale and come back down to earth, I will share my advice on how to have a beautiful, tasteful, memorable, and STRESS FREE wedding in well under a year. You probably think I'm drunk if I'm using the words "stress-free" and "wedding" in the same sentence. Well, I can assure you that I haven't had a drink all morning and I can confidently say that it's possible.

I want to make it clear that I love weddings. As a wedding planner it's kind of my job to. Do not mistake this book for a hater's guide to the ultimate wedding bashing. It's quite the opposite. I've planned dozens of weddings and I've met dozens of brides;

some beautiful ones and some not so beautiful ones (and I'm not talking about on the outside). I've seen broken engagements, broken friendships and families torn apart as a result of this one day everyone puts so much emphasis on. Is it really worth it? A wedding shouldn't be about competition and showing off what's no longer in your bank account and it certainly shouldn't be treated as a two year business venture. It should be about you and your partner and should reflect you both as individuals as well as a couple. It should be a fun and exciting celebration of the life you're about to share together. No, I don't think you should just get married in a church basement and eat out of take-out containers just because its only one day - unless that truly is a representation of you then all the power to you! This one day is special. It's special because it's unique to you and your story. And most importantly your timeline and your budget.

The first thing you need to do after you've announced your engagement is sit down with your partner and assess your situation. So many factors come into play when deciding on a date. It could be a bun in the oven, a law degree still in the works, an around the world trip, or a million other commitments you may have. You need to consider all these things and you need to prioritize. To some, the moment they get engaged, the wedding gets put at the top of that priority list. If that's you then you're lucky. A lot of us aren't that fortunate.

2

If I did it...

HOW WE STAYED GROUNDED

When I got engaged I was in an unusual situation. I was living with my now husband in Melbourne, Australia. We got engaged in January of 2013 and were married in July 2013 in Toronto. When he popped the question he was in the middle of a huge renovation with one of his investment properties. We were preparing for our move to Toronto which was quickly approaching in April and our house was a complete nightmare. I basically had to pack an entire house into twelve boxes to throw on a crate and ship to Canada. At the same time, I had seven months to plan our wedding with four of those months being on the other side of the world. I had a choice. I could let this wedding consume my life or I could manage my time with what really mattered;

spending it with the friends and family we would be leaving behind in a few short months. In between we managed to nut out the details of our upcoming wedding and pop over to Fiji on the way to our new home. I know it sounds impossible, but, it's not. We decided to be sensible. We made our choices revolve around us, our friends, family and our budget. Not around the latest trend.

I'm sure you're asking why we rushed to the end of the altar. A few reasons. It was very important for us to get married in the summer. We had intentions of honeymooning in Europe but more significantly we wanted our Aussie friends and family to experience Canada in the summer. Bringing a bunch of Aussies to snow, we thought, would not be a good idea. Another reason was they didn't actually believe that we did, in fact, have summer in Canada. With the seasons and school years being opposite we had a very small window with dates, so the only time everyone was on holidays was the first two weeks of July. No part of me was bummed because I couldn't get married on some significant date like 11/11/11. Despite contrary belief, the wedding date does not determine happiness and good fortune. Then came the hard part: the venue. How do you possibly lock in a venue from another continent? Reviews, people. Reviews and referrals. Who cares if someone you know was married there? You need to know that the food and service is outstanding since you're not there to do the tasting yourself. We shortlisted about twenty venues that needed minimal decor and that were within our budget in the city of Toronto and then started making contact. This is the part you need to spend a bit of time on. You need to shortlist (it really should be called longlist) quite a few venues when you have such specific requests; like a date only seven months away. And the even harder part, you cannot be picky. We didn't have the luxury to turn a place down because we didn't like the colour of the linens. This is where we made another choice. We had the option to wait until the next summer - which would mean being engaged for 19 months - and having our (my) dream wedding or we could kick the superficial crap out the window and find a venue that would tick two of our very important boxes - food and minimal decor - so we could start our lives together sooner. We chose door number two. This is where people usually make the mistake and it snowballs into a nightmare. It's a lot harder to go with sensibility than you think.

We called our twenty or so venues and after a few gasps of "SEVEN months??? We don't have availability until 2016!" we narrowed it down to three venues that were available and suited our needs. This is where my family in Toronto came in and acted as my senses. My parents and my sister visited the venues and came back to me with the pros and cons. I was confident that after 28 years they knew me well enough to make a decision on my behalf. This is where lesson number two comes in. Don't be a control freak. Was it frustrating that I had never stepped foot into the venue I'd be dishing 40% of my budget into? Of course. Could I do anything about it? No. So rather than stomp around asking daddy to fly me home so I could plan my wedding I let them help me. After all, I was knee deep in boxes packing up our Melbourne home.

I promised myself - and everyone else who's sick of hearing it - that I would not make this book about me and I don't intend to. But I will give you a little insight into our story and why my wedding day was not the be all and end all of my relationship.

My hubby and I met in passing on the Greek Islands. His first day, my last day, we hit it off, we had one of the best nights of my life with the friends we were with and said that we'd be seeing each other again. We had no idea how or when but we just knew. Very cliché. We kept in contact while he travelled the world and he detoured to Toronto while visiting New York a month or so later. This is where we put things into overdrive. We weren't two star-crossed teenagers who wanted to uproot their lives and be together forever but we knew that what we had was too strong to let go. We also knew that long distance relationships just don't work. This may open a whole new can of worms for your Book Club but that's a different story. With our financial situations, work commitments and lack of vacation days it just wouldn't be feasible to see each other every six months. This was Melbourne to Toronto remember, not Toronto to New York. Not to mention, we weren't getting any younger. We said, ' let's go for it'. I was finishing up wedding season and had a lot more flexibility than he did. I could pick up my company and run it from anywhere in the world. I made that sound easy; it wasn't. But if one of us was going to do something insane it had to be me. I shocked my family and friends and I moved to Melbourne on a working holiday visa in the new year. Just four months after we had met and after only spending 48 hours together in person. In hindsight, I can see why everyone was so uneasy about this and why my parents freaked. As an expecting mom now, I think about my kid uprooting to the other side of the world for a complete stranger and it makes me want to puke.

It was only meant to be for six months. Six months later Mark came back to Toronto with me to meet my loved ones, so they could see that he wasn't a total psychopath, and we went back to Melbourne for what turned into three years.

There is a point to this love story and it's one simple fact. It changed me. It grounded me. It showed me what really matters in life and how hard it can be. Before I uprooted my life and turned both our worlds upside down, the hardest decision I ever dealt with seemed miniscule compared to the life changing decisions I was now dealing with. I was homesick, I was missing my family, I was trying to start a business, and I was new to a city where I had only his world, his family, and his friends to lean on. I had no idea what the future held and was scared to death that I had made a huge mistake. After all, I moved to the other side of the world for a man I knew for four minutes.

If it worked, where would we live? What would happen? What if we had kids then divorced and I was stuck in Melbourne? Or him in Toronto? What if something happens to someone back home? I'm so far away. How is this going to work? Well, after a rollercoaster of emotions and two years later, everything seemed clearer and I counted my blessings every day. I was lucky. I still am. I am living a real life fairytale. Prince Charming didn't turn out to be a serial killer (totally could have gone that way). Now I was getting married to him. And he was not only getting married in Toronto but moving to the other side of the world for ME. I was overwhelmed with happiness. And stress. Wedding planning, job hunting and packing up our home and moving - which is known to be the three most stressful times in a couple's life (minus catastrophes of course) - were all thrown at us at once. Can you see why the wedding details didn't matter so much now?

Despite all the noise, I still had a super cool wedding if I don't say so myself. Awesome venue, amazing food, and an incredible party. I also managed to have everything done, dusted, signed, sealed and delivered by the time everyone came over three weeks before the wedding. The weeks leading up were spent touring the city and showing my Aussies why I love Toronto. This also gave me a chance to fall in love with my city all over again after being away for so long. We went to Niagara Falls, Muskoka for a weekend so they could experience our "cottage living", we went to numerous restaurants, rooftop patios, guided tours, all the main attractions and even a couple of sporting events. If I was too wrapped up in my wedding details I would have never had the opportunity to do this with everyone. That was my priority. The memories we made in those days leading up to the wedding were far more precious to me than minor wedding details that no one would notice.

The one thing that did take us ages was the music selection. We are very passionate about our music, Mark is very passionate about his dance moves, and this is what we focused on for the majority of our engagement.

Scan this BARCODE to check out our music selections! Great for playlist ideas - the dance floor was full all night!

Think about it: Why would you hire all those vendors if you're planning on taking over and doing everything yourself? The florist took care of the flowers, the venue took care of the food and everyone else their jobs while the wedding planner took care of the last minute details. They're the experts. Yes, I'm a wedding planner and fully capable of executing my own or anyone else's wedding - but why should I? Why would I want to be running around when I could be spending time with the people I love who made a huge effort to watch me say I DO! We took over the music to cut costs, hence choosing a DJ who was a friend that charged us next to nothing. We were happy to select every song because it was fun and it was something we did together. It didn't break the bank nor did it break us and to this day I take pride in hearing, "your wedding was still the best wedding I've ever been to." If I ask that person about the centerpieces though, they won't remember. And I couldn't care less. In the end I had my dream wedding and I didn't break the bank or break a sweat.

Over the past decade I've learned about different cultures, lifestyles and traditions and developed a passion for beautifully organized events. From one side of the world to the other, my travelling experiences have lead me to pick up amazing tips and trends and effortlessly put together weddings that each have an individual and unique touch according to their particular budget. If you want a six figure wedding I can tell you about those too, but this book isn't about that. I'm not saying those weddings aren't worth the money spent. It's all relative. Couples who plan six figure weddings can still be sensible. If you can afford it, go for it. I'm simply saying don't plan something for the sake of putting on a show that you can't afford to pay for later just to impress those you don't really give a shit about. Why do we buy shit we don't need with money we don't have, to impress people we don't like, anyway?

Living overseas and turning my whole world upside down grounded me and taught me what really mattered. It's not all about the main event. It's the lead up and the road to follow that you need to pay more attention to. I wrote this book because although I love weddings, I believe they've derailed from representing a love and connection between two people and a celebration of the start of the rest of their lives together. Many weddings are now about who can put on the most expensive show or who can get featured in the most exclusive blog and it's become so off-putting. Besides, these blogs are just full of show ponies who, in my opinion, don't have real friends of their own.

I hope you enjoy this book as much as I enjoyed writing it. I hope you take something from it and have the most amazing engagement, wedding and marriage you can possibly have.

Bessy xo

3

The Budget

PLAN FOR WHAT YOU CAN AFFORD

I know the feeling all too well. You just said yes and you're on a massive high. You want the wedding of your dreams and hey, what's $60,000? You're getting cash gifts, so why not spend the next year treating your wedding as a business and see how much money you can suck out of your guests to subsidize your big day. Right? Wrong.. So, so wrong. Firstly, this is a gross way of looking at things and secondly, no one ever makes money off of their wedding! A typical meal with a full host bar may cost between $100-$200 per person but when you factor in your photographer, decor, stationery, entertainment and everything else in between, you're doubling that figure at the very least. If you think your guests will cover that in their monetary gifts then please email me your guest lists because I'd love to have these people at my parties. My 30th is just around the corner.

As tempting as that sounds, when you're planning your budget you need to do it with zero expectations of your guests helping you foot the bill. Think about it from your guests perspective. The first thing they think when they get that invite in the mail is not "oh how pretty". It's "Shit, another wedding, at this venue they're probably paying $160 per person, can we afford that?" It's sickening. This isn't a fundraiser. People shouldn't be expected to pay a cover charge. If that's the case, you may as well hire a bouncer.

Sit down with your fiancé and start crunching your numbers based on what YOU can afford. It would be wise to get a wedding planner to help with this. You tell them what you can afford and they will give you a line by line breakdown of how to allocate those funds. Many people think that hiring a wedding planner is a luxury but it's not - it's a necessity. Our job as wedding planners is to keep you within your budget. We incorporate our charge in your budget so you don't feel it and most importantly we keep you within it. More than two thirds of couples go over budget on their weddings according to a 2013 survey from Weddingbells Magazine which polled 2200 readers. 30% over to be exact. Considering that huge inflation, don't you think it's worth letting a wedding planner take up 15% of your budget and keep you from going over? When you look at it that way it's pretty clear that that would be the way to go. These couples who go over budget become desperate to gain back some money and they do unacceptable things like add a little poem to their invite that "politely" asks for monetary gifts. We'll circle back to this in the *Tacky Wedding Etiquette* chapter of this book.

Before you start sourcing out planners you need to decide on a magic number. This is where you need to be sensible. The average engagement period is one year and eleven months. That's a long time and gives you a lot of time to inflate your budget. Pick a date within nine months if you know what's good for you. Always remember that for the duration of your engagement you're on cloud nine. The day after the wedding you're still floating around up there and that will last for about a week. Your helium will start to run out as notifications on Facebook and Instagram of photos and congratulatory messages subside and you're back down to Earth with the bill. You've got nothing left from your wedding gifts because rather than spending that money on your future, your home renos or your honeymoon, you've tried to bring down the wedding debt. Now what are you going to do?

Too many couples have this huge party, show off and then expect everyone else to help fund it. That's not what it's about. This is not your business it's your wedding! If you can't afford it, don't do it. It's very straightforward. There's absolutely nothing wrong with not having the money to put on such an elaborate event. I may sound like I'm anti wedding and I'm certainly not. But I'm anti "exhaust all resources, drain your credit cards and put yourself into debt so you can show off something you don't have just to keep up with the latest trends" I know it's hard not to get starry eyed and discouraged when sites like Pinterest and Etsy are showcasing all the latest expensive trends but you can't lose sight of what your wedding is about. These sites are not out there to rub it in your face they're out there to make money. If you can't afford it just look at alternatives. Don't succumb to the pressure.

What you're idolizing, ladies, is all bullshit anyway. It's not real. These brides are going into debt, putting their parents into debt, dumping their wedding gifts into the budget just to live the lifestyle you crave. Most of them have nothing, it's all smoke and mirrors.

That's another thing that makes me crazy. These girls who pollute Facebook and Instagram with all things their wedding just to say "look how rich I am" meanwhile they have not a penny to their names and are still living and mooching off of their parents. They're showing off their parent's hard work and passing it off as their own. If it wasn't for mommy and daddy working around the clock saving for their children's' weddings and educations (something none of us can brag about) every one of those brides would be going to City Hall followed by dinner at McDonalds - Two can Dine for $9.99 for their wedding reception. I'm not saying there's anything wrong with this. If I could go back I WOULD go to McDonald's. Or at least bring in cheeseburgers and McChickens for the late night station. Don't get me wrong, I loved my wedding. I still love my wedding. I look back at the photos and I get goose bumps. That mushy gushy feeling though, isn't from gawking over the centerpieces. It's from looking back at the love and laughter and reliving the memories of the day. Regardless of the stuff that surrounded my wedding day, all that mattered was that I married my best friend and was starting the next chapter of my life.

Let me break down the budget for you. Regardless of whether your budget is $4000 or $40000, this will help put things into perspective.

Let's start with the bulk of your funds. Feeding and replenishing your guests. For the reception/ceremony and catering you should typically be spending between 35-40% of your total budget. This is a huge chunk and there are some factors to consider to stick within it.

Still struggling to make ends meet and literally don't know what else to downsize? How about your guest list? Coming from a big Fat Greek Family and marrying into an even bigger fatter Italian one, I know a thing or two about never ending guest lists. Starting with, they're unnecessary. One of my brides is a perfect example of this. I'm doing her invites, place cards, table numbers, menus and thank you tags. Guess how many people she's having at her wedding? SIX HUNDRED. Are you seriously kidding me? Naturally, I asked her why the hell she was hosting so many goddamn people.

"Because I have to"

"Um, no you don't. What the hell do you mean you have to? You're telling me you are obligated to have that many people at your wedding. Have all these 600 people met both you and you're fiancé?"

"Well, no. But…"

"Ok, so cut the ones you've never met. Moving on. When was the last time you saw these 600 people. Can you confidently say that you have seen them all within the last 6 months to a year?"

"Well, no. But…"

"No. No but's. You don't HAVE to do anything."

Despite how this conversation begun, or how it ended, yes I still did her stationary. I still did it for 600 people. What boggled my mind was how the second I gave her a quote she panicked with the figures. My prices are pretty reasonable. It wasn't that. It was the $5.50 per invite x 400 households! Not to mention the postage that wasn't included in my pricing. She tried to cut corners with cheaper paper and one sided printing, only got one menu per table instead of two and didn't want anything beyond basic. She even asked me if I could just give her the place cards and she'd handwrite them. That's where I drew the line. Nothing with my name on it goes out handwritten and sloppy. Not a chance. Not unless it's written in calligraphy and professionally done. Point is, she had a vision in mind and she was pretty disappointed when I couldn't give her exactly what she wanted on her budget. All she had to do was consider knocking out 100 people off of her guest list and there's $550 right there she would have had to play with. If she knocked off 200 people she would have saved $1100 and would STILL have a 400 person guest list. Not to mention everywhere else she'd save on the smaller count.

If you're not willing to put the money into everything for every guests then start cutting people. Your day should be the way you want it. Not controlled by the guests you're inviting and what you're obligated to pay for them.

Anyone that says they HAVE to invite that many people is lying. What kind of bullshit is that? If you're inviting that many, don't act like you don't want to. I don't get the whole huge guest list wedding thing, anyway. I may get some heat on this but if I haven't seen or spoken to you in the last six months you have no business at my wedding. Yes, there are the people your parents want to invite that you may have never met, and if you're a traditional Greek Orthodox for example, it's customary for the "koumbaro" (best man) to invite a table of his own as it's also his celebration. But those extra few guests do not add up to the hundreds so take your bullshit somewhere else and sell it.

And do you think these people you're inviting want to be invited? Do you know how many invites I've gotten where I thought, "Why the hell am I invited to this? I don't even know this person." Trust me, by making some cuts you're not only doing yourself a favor, chances are you're doing them a favor as well.

Some might say they're getting some serious slack from their parents and are being pressured to invite certain people that they've never met because if they don't, "what will people say?". I totally get this as we dealt with this as well. Word of advice, your parents won't disown you. I'm not saying screw your parents and don't let them invite anyone. But when they're taking control of the guest list and your count goes from 200 to 400 you need to draw the line. Give them two tables and tell them to choose accordingly. They can simply tell their friends there wasn't enough room. Those friends of theirs will not talk shit, they probably won't even care. And if they do, you made the right decision cutting them out to begin with.

There are some people that treat their wedding like a business from day one. They try and pack 600 people into a banquet hall just to collect their gifts, so they can pay that hall and have some money left over. First, this is gross and embarrassing. Second, you never make money off your wedding anyway! Seriously, if you're running low on funds, get a second job, cut back on the take-out or stop living beyond your means. But please do not treat your wedding day as another source of income. If you can't afford to host two, three, four or five hundred people at your wedding then cut your list down to what you can afford.

Besides the venues for the reception and ceremony, the rest of the budget goes like this:

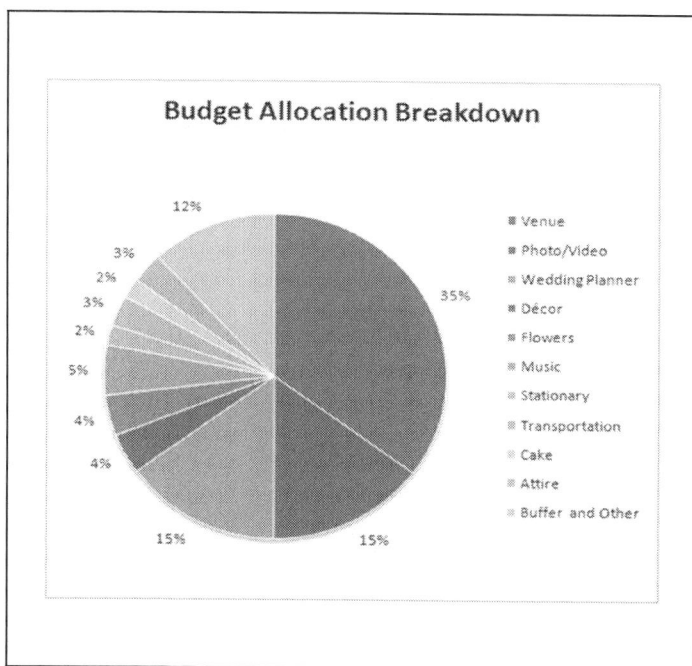

Budget Allocation Breakdown

- Venue — 35%
- Photo/Video — 15%
- Wedding Planner — 15%
- Décor
- Flowers
- Music
- Stationary
- Transportation
- Cake
- Attire
- Buffer and Other
- 12%, 3%, 2%, 3%, 2%, 5%, 4%, 4%

Some budgets will vary. This is the breakdown I used and what I pass along to my clients. Feel free to jumble numbers around as every wedding budget is different. This process can also be a bit fun. Say your uncle is a photographer and wants to shoot your wedding as your wedding gift and you accept, BAM there's 15% of your funds you can either save or put where you need it. Scan the barcode below and in BeLaV's budget template you can amend the figures to be whatever percentage you'd like to allocate where. If you start here, it will take you down the stress free path. Trust me.

Scan this BARCODE to see BeLaV's easy wedding budget planner

4

Cut the Crap

FROM THE VENUE TO THE DÉCOR: WHAT
YOU DON'T NEED

On a super short timeline, you can't have
everything. First things first: Pick a date. Yes, despite
contrary belief, choosing a date first seriously helps
eliminate some stress. The worst thing you can do is
say I'm going to let the venue determine the date.
This is how people end up in three year engagements
because they spend six months looking for the
PERFECT VENUE but it's not available until 2018.
If you choose the date first then you'll have a lot less
to weigh up. Now, don't take this completely literally.
If you find a great venue, you fall head over heels in
love, it ticks all your boxes and you can be flexible
with your date, then by all means switch it up. If
you're looking at April 17th but they only have the
24th available don't hang up and never look back. Just

have a solid idea of when you want to get married. Additionally, it's still very important to have a couple of back up dates within a few weeks of each other. You'll have to do a bit of back and forth with ceremony and reception venues if they're not in one location.

Next...Numbers numbers numbers! Are you having a small intimate wedding or a Broadway production? Also, who's the majority that will be attending? What financial situations and what commitments do your loved ones have? If your bestie is at home with her 3 year old then she may not be able to haul ass to Bali for a barefoot wedding on the beach. Neither will grandma. How important is this to you? If you're not a selfish cow, I'm going to say it's pretty important. Of course you won't be able to please everyone and it is your day, but it will be worth considering these details if it means your nearest and dearest can be there to witness you become a Mrs.

Let's continue with the basics: A ceremony venue, a reception venue and some delish catering. For your sanity, try and have all three at the same location. For those of you who want to get married in a religious institution then I highly recommend when choosing the ceremony and reception venue try and keep them as close together as possible. This isn't only convenient for you when you're going from one place to the next, it maximizes your photo ops time and it's convenient for your guests as well. While you're cruising around in your limo drinking champagne, they're stuck in traffic, taking public transport from one end of the city to the other or hopping in and out of cabs. The last thing you want to do is send them on the Tour de France.

When starting your hunt, think about what's more important to you. Ceremony or reception. Of course, both equally important but for narrowing it down you need to start somewhere. Are you more concerned about marrying in a stunning downtown cathedral with gorgeous stained glass windows, high ceilings and an incredibly spectacular long aisle? Then start your research here. Find the perfect one and then you have a handful of venues to choose from that are nearby for the party. Get your map out and if it's not within your radius then move it along. If you're happy to marry anywhere but are set on a reception venue that ticks all your boxes then start your research here. See if they have a ceremony location on site (most do) or find something nearby. Beaches or parks are great locations for neutral ceremonies. They require a few chairs and limited decor as they have the priceless scenery surrounding them so aside from a permit, it's pretty easy to find somewhere fitting.

Choosing the perfect venue can be a bit overwhelming and it requires a bit more time than everything else. This is where the bulk of your budget is going so you don't want to just pick anything. I'm sensible, I'm not irrational. The GTA alone has over 1000 known wedding venues. This doesn't include the unconventional ones that aren't listed as "wedding venues" so let's add another 200 to that list. You're not going to see them all. Here's how it's going to go. Sit down with your Mr. and have a look at your budget. Take 40% of it and that's what you should be spending on the venue and catering. You need to consider if the pricing is based on room rental, per person minimum spend or if there are set packages.

Next, choose a style. Sit down, cocktail, brunch, formal, informal, etc. This should have already cut down your options significantly. That's what you want. Less options means less confusion. Think about what you want from your wedding venue. I'm a spreadsheet kind of girl. Create one or use mine HERE: Feel free to add or remove tabs according to your requirements.

This lists all the important points you're looking for, allowing you to keep track of each venue's suitability as you do your research.

Do an online search and start with a long list of venues you like the look of in your chosen geographical area before contacting them for more info. That list is getting shorter and shorter as you're considering these important factors: For example, with capacity, you aren't expected to know your headcount this early on but before contacting anyone you should definitely have an idea. Keeping in mind you may have to be willing to cut or add guests if the venue has a minimum or maximum guest requirement.

Other things to consider are is there an outdoor space and is that important to you? It shouldn't be if you're living in Toronto because weather may not be on your side. You could be wondering if there are any other weddings going on the same day. This is important to some and not so important to others. In my opinion it's nice to know you're the only bride onsite. If you're considering using a lot of candles for décor, it's important to know if there are any open flame restrictions. When meeting with a venue and their coordinators in the early stages you're not discussing your décor ideas in detail so this may get overlooked. Then before you know it you've booked, they don't allow candles and your whole idea for intimate and inexpensive lighting is out the window. Finally, are there any added fees such as a landmark or historic fee? You have to be careful with historical buildings. Although they are timeless and absolutely stunning, there are a lot of hidden fees to take into consideration. This may be a make or break because some of these fees can be in the thousands, so don't fall in love just yet as it may be out of your budget.

Scan this BARCODE for BeLaV's Venue Checklist

Once you've gone through this list of crap and crossed one venue off after another, your magic number should now be around 15-20. Quite a dip from the thousand you started with, right? See, not so overwhelming after all so you can start calming down.

Moving on. Choose your theme. This is imperative. I know Gatsby is hot right now and rustic was so last season, but in 5 minutes it's going to be the other way around. Then it's going to change again. This is where you have to do it the traditional way. Turn off all electronics and mobile devices and come up with a style that reflects you and your other half. Whether it be rustic, vintage, art deco, grunge, Star Wars (yes I've seen it - and yes it was awesome) or elegant and Victorian, make sure it's a true representation of you. You have no idea how many brides I've had, who by the time they got their wedding albums, hated everything about their weddings because they went with the latest trends which disappeared faster than Gangnam Style.

Catering is a big one. If your reception venue has it then fantastic. Major tick in my books. If they don't then you'll have to do a lot more leg work and this is where you get into a lot more hidden costs. There's a good chance your venue has a preferred list of suppliers. If that's the case then they'll also have a penalty fee if you don't use them. They could have contracts with the top five caterers in your city but you were going to opt for a less expensive one. Well, you're shit out of luck because the venue will then slap a 20% fee for using someone outside their "preferred list". It should be called mandatory list because it's pretty unjustifiable going with someone else under those circumstances.

When you take this penalty into consideration for the tables, chairs, linens, centerpieces, DJ and all your other suppliers then you'll realize those figures add up to that pair of Alexander McQueen's you've been eyeing that you thought you couldn't afford. Now that you're expected to pay that on literally nothing then I think it's time to revisit your venue list and then pop over to Holt Renfrew to spend your money on those shoes that aren't looking so bad after all. My advice, and you'll thank me for it, go with a venue that has it all. Most reception venues are equipped with full kitchens and excellent chefs. Spend a little more on a reputable venue; trust me it'll be worth it. You need to consider things like: are you looking for more traditional options? Can they cater to yours and your guests tastes? If you have a big fat European family then you know they'll be expecting to see a very large antipasto bar as soon as they walk in.

Next order of business you'll need to consider when nailing down your venue. Decor. So much hassle and stress can go out the window when you choose a venue that requires minimal decor. I know you have your heart set on that empty barn 40 kilometers outside of town but you'll get over it pretty quickly when you are the one that has to clear out the hay, haul in the tables, arrange for glorified Porta-Potties, arrange for lighting, a dance floor, catering, piping, draping, and more importantly, masking that lovely stench of horse shit. There's also the weather to keep in mind. If you're from my two homes, Melbourne or Toronto where you get four seasons in one day and you're planning an outdoor ceremony or reception, you'll need a backup plan in the case of rain or snow, which means twice as much stress.

See what I'm saying? A reception hall or wedding venue will be well equipped with staff to take care of the dirty work for you, which will definitely include post wedding clean up. Who the hell wants to clean up after their wedding? I wanted to do one thing and one thing only when the lights came on. Get the hell out of my dress and pee. Everyone starts off by saying, "I don't want a 'hall'. It's so 'wedding-y'. I want something unique." Yeah, yeah, I've heard it many times before and I said it myself. If you're willing to dig deep into your pockets for an art gallery or barn or anything with an bare roof and exposed brick then go for it. But that's what unique means. If you want an unconventional wedding space be willing to pay big bucks for it. There's no way around it. If you don't want to shell out the cash for it then get over it.

We chose a venue that barely needed a thing. All in with a premium bar we spent $170 per person. Did that number make you cringe? Have a guess what our decor cost. About $5 per person. This included centerpieces, table decor, candles, place cards, a seating chart and all our other decor like a few canvases we had hanging with love quotes. Prior to choosing our venue we sent our family to another venue just outside the city that was charging $135 per person. This venue offered all the same things in terms of food and beverage selections. The only difference was that it was a room with a couple of chandeliers. Nothing more to it. Our venue had exposed ceilings with modern light fixtures, a bar on the dance floor with this incredible art deco mirror and this insanely cool damask patterned wallpaper on one wall. They had heaps of black and white contemporary lounge furniture and an incredible parlor for the cocktail hour. It was sensational. Besides mine and my girls' bouquets there was not a flower in the place on my wedding day. Don't get me wrong, flowers would have looked awesome. About $10,000 worth of flowers. I love them, but I don't love them that much. Anything else would have been swallowed up by the room and quite frankly I didn't think the room needed them. It was super cool as is. And if flowers aren't done right, they shouldn't be done at all. Simple. No one noticed anyway. People notice when they're elaborate and in your face when they walk in. Flowers can give that major wow factor. People also notice when they look like crap. What people can't notice is something that isn't there. No one was saying, hey where are the flowers?? They were saying, 'Holy shit check out that mirror!'

They were paying attention to the table numbers which were each named after a literary couple followed by a famous quote from their story. Those cost next to nothing as I designed and created them myself. They were paying attention to the mini typewriters we used as place card holders with a little thank you for travelling xxx amount of kilometers to spend our special day with us. Those cost $0.30 each. They noticed the mini notebook and bookmark with a personalized Thank You message. They noticed the canvases with quotes from classic love stories hung around the room and they noticed the long table of photos of those that have either passed on or couldn't make the trip to the other side of the world to be with us. They especially noticed the songs we selected which had the dance floor packed for six hours straight. We spent the most amount of time picking each and every song that was played because we love to dance and so do our friends and family. Our wedding wasn't about the biggest and the best of everything. It was about what and who we love. I love to write and I live for happy endings so the literary theme was perfectly fitting. We were beyond grateful to have 30 people from Melbourne trek to the other side of the world to come to our wedding like we were royalty so we thanked them in every way we possibly could. These are the things I can proudly say that our dearest still talk about. They cost nothing; they just came from the heart. We had no piping and draping. Although it looks pretty beautiful to pimp out the head table, I didn't see why my table should be any nicer than my guests tables. This just seemed silly to me. A lot of people stress that it's important to differentiate your table to everyone else's so the guests know where you are. Umm, pretty sure I'm the one with the big white dress in the center of the room. What more do people need to distinguish who I am? I do not need to be elevated and I do not need all kinds of draping and spotlighting around me. I'm not royalty.

Banquet halls aren't as tacky as they use to be. Most venues are up with the times and are looking more and more modern. As long as you're not choosing one that was built and last renovated in 1987 then you've got everything you need in one place with a reasonable price tag. If you pay a little bit more then you can find a pretty distinctive one.

Back to the less expensive reception hall. It would have needed some serious decor. We would have had to pipe and drape the shit out of it. Lighting needed to be brought it and it needed a forest of flowers. When we went back and got out our calculators we worked out our decor in total would have cost another $62 per person. Yes, that's $197 per person for the venue and decor all up, 30 kilometers outside of the city. Our venue had a local inner city area code (416) so it was central and was $22 cheaper per person. We skipped the pipe and draping, skipped the flowers, went with black lanterns of all sizes and heaps of white candles - we axed the unnecessary chair covers, because did I forget to mention our venue had chiavari chairs?

This brings me to my next point. If you don't like the tables, chairs, linens or any other decor the venue offers then just cut your losses and choose another one. You don't find a partner, say to yourself he'll do I'll just change everything about him and then he'll be perfect! (actually some people do) So you shouldn't do it with any of the decisions you make. There's one thing I hate when it comes to wedding decor. Yes, hate. It's a pretty bold statement, but I hate chair covers. One, they're hideous and two, they are the biggest waste of money. But more so, because they're hideous. If your venue has ugly chairs either deal with it or move along to a different one. Some have gotten with the times and have chiavari or ghost chairs that come standard; others haven't because they figure they can make a few extra bucks by providing you with the ugliest satin material to cover them up. They also have an array of colours which they can match to their tacky napkins and linens. Just don't do it. I'd rather deal with the ugly chairs.

I'm getting a little off topic here, but the point is try to eliminate as much added crap as you can. None of it matters and what most people don't realize is that it all adds up. They start with a budget of $120 per person and book a place thinking they've gotten the deal of the century but end up spending just as much per person giving the place a makeover. It's very easy to get caught up in the emotion of it all, walk into a venue, the price is right, you fall in love and you sign on the dotted line. Then, you come to realize all the add-ons and hidden costs. It's very important to consider all the logistics. Don't overlook the slightly pricier venues right away. You may be paying more per head but you'll end up spending less if they have most things in house. And if they're pricey and in the city and have a good reputation then at least you know you're getting quality. When you see chair covers and matching satin linens then you're probably also getting frozen food. No one that charges $100 per person is serving anything fresh, sorry ladies.

Scan this BARCODE to see our wedding crap-free checklist!

Here are a couple of things that you can cut out that no one will notice:

The linens - self explanatory.

What kind of flowers you used - I'm not saying ditch the flowers all together. I'm just saying that you don't have to get the most expensive ones. If you're doing huge floral bouquets, the actual flowers don't matter. All that matters is the colour you want and how full they are. A huge bunch of white assorted less expensive flowers will look much more expensive than a smaller bunch of roses. Or, dare I say it? Use fake flowers! When you have a three foot centerpiece and you just need a ball of roses to sit on top of it you can just get super cheap rose balls that look super real. You can either keep them, you can give them away, or you can sell them. Either way, who cares, they were cheap.

The really expensive flutes you cheers with:

These are pointless. We had Vera Wang ones. Some people spend hundreds on a couple glasses that end up in a couple pictures that end up looking like normal champagne glasses the venue could have provided. Don't sweat these and splurge somewhere else.

Bouquet toss/garter toss:

You might think it's a cute tradition to appoint and embarrass the single ladies at your wedding by making them stand in the middle of the room where everyone can see them and then proceed to launch your bouquet to Queen Bey's super annoying tune "All the Single Ladies". My guess is you've spent a pretty penny on this bouquet or on a "throw-away" to destroy it on a bunch of women who go all Hunger Games on each other and completely shame themselves further. There's hair pulling, dress ripping, make-up smudging, straight up pushing and shoving, just to get their pretty little hands on some flowers that apparently determine their romantic futures. I'd go all Karate Kid on them as well if I thought that bouquet was my last chance at true love. Once that one lucky lady succeeds she emerges from the pile-up and cheers as though she's just won the Stanley Cup. She locks eyes with the dude that caught the garter and immediately goes all "Stage 5 Clinger" on him. After her public display of humiliation he can't get further away from her while she's already picturing their wedding and her bouquet toss in a few short months where she'll get the thrill of feeling superior to her friends and family because now she's the one that's getting married and doesn't have to fear a long and lonely life. This is a completely ludicrous tradition and no one will notice that it didn't go down – except for the single ladies who are quietly thanking you for not putting them through such mortification.

5

Choosing Your Vendors

You could go down the 'List' of those sought after blogs and pay and arm and a leg for those vendors who also have paid an arm and a leg to advertize on those very sites. Or you can be reasonable and forget the who's who in the wedding world because they've got more money to advertize and go for the passionate under the radar vendors who would beyond appreciate your business. Those are the ones that will do a spectacular job without the spectacular price tag for one simple reason. OK two reasons. They are grateful for your business and they love what they do. These are the up and coming Lister's so best to get on them ASAP. You may be wondering what this 'List' is that I am talking about. If you're still with me by the Competition chapter (chapter 7) you'll get an earful about it. The List is not a contributing factor to choosing your vendors in my opinion which is why I won't elaborate until we get there.

Before I fill you in on how to find your vendors, here's how not to find them: if they are friends with you or related to you. NEVER use friends or family. I find myself telling this to everyone and no one listens. Then they come back to me and say, "Bess, I should have listened to you." You think??

A perfect example of this is one of my last years' clients. We'll call her Vicky. Vicky needed her invites designed and printed on the cheap. I offered up my services as I'm just starting in the Invite World and don't charge nearly as much as the going rate. She still thought my rates were too expensive and out of her budget (which they weren't) so she ventured off into the world to find someone cheaper. She succeeded and went ahead and locked in one of her friends who designed them for free. All she had to pay for was printing. She called me a few days later and let me in on her accomplishment. Great! I thought. "Can you send me one to look over before you send them off?" I had asked her. "Nope, too late." She said. "They've been signed, sealed and delivered! Can't believe I got them out in time!"

A few days later, low and behold there was the invite in my mailbox. After about half a second of scanning the invite and thinking, "OK, not bad..." I gasped in utter disbelief. There was no venue location on the invitation. No location! How the hell has my phone not gone off the hook?? And just like that, Vicky's name appeared on my phone. Here we go. She cried and screamed and demanded a solution to this completely unfixable issue. It's not like I could go to all 240 households and write the venue in for them. She was practically hyperventilating on the other end of the line and as I tried to calm her down she just got more excited as she had emails, texts and calls coming through her other line. The only thing we could do was send out another little card with a cutesy poem and where the wedding was being held ASAP. I told her to shut her phone off and just get out of town to chill out in the meantime while trying really hard not to say I FUCKING TOLD YOU SO! Needless to say, this little mistake cost her far more than what she tried to save on her half-assed invitations. At the very least if an online paper shop or any other professional made this unacceptable mistake she would have gotten a full refund and then some. In this case she got a mumbled, "I'm sorry" from her 'friend' and a swift kick in the ass. She lost a friend, lost some valuable time and a lot more money than she had planned to spend.

There are two lessons to learn from this nightmare. ALWAYS listen to your wedding planner and NEVER hire your friends or family. There are many more reasons not to deal with your loved ones when it comes to your wedding. I know they'll be cheaper (if they do it right) but that's the only plus. If you don't like something or they may be taking their sweet-ass time on something you need ASAP, it's hard to demand things on your timeline. After all, they are doing you a favour. When someone is doing you a favour then unfortunately it's almost always on their agenda and not yours. You are not their priority you're just their cousin that they're helping out in their spare time. Even if it does work out in the end you never have control of the situation and it's just not worth the headache. You don't want to be someone's number ten, you want to be right up there with their priorities so you know they're not doing half a job just because you're paying half the money. However, the main reason not to hire someone you know is that if shit hits the fan, there's really nothing anyone can do about it. They can't give you your money back because you've barely paid for anything, you can't really rip them a new one because of the whole family thing and chances are you'll ruin what once was a great relationship. Just don't go there.

Another avenue not to go down is the internet. Yes, I'm telling you to ditch the technology and go old school on this one. Do you know how draining and overwhelming it is to type "Toronto Wedding Photographer" into Google and get 56,986 results? Who the hell has time to go through all those? You'll go through maybe three to four pages. And then you'll give up. The ones on the first few pages are not

44

the best they just have deep pockets. And their prices are through the roof. They also have great marketing teams. They make their websites super appealing and that's what makes you justify upping your photography budget from $3,000 to $10,000. Stay away from the internet as long as you can or until you try my suggestions.

Blogs use to be a great way to find vendors but sites like Style Me Pretty and Wedluxe have gotten so huge now with social media that they too charge insane amounts of money for advertizing. They're not featuring weddings on their blogs anymore because they're pretty and unique. They're taking the highest bidder. If I as a wedding planner pay them $4000 a year to advertize with them then of course they're going to feature one or two of my weddings on their blog just to keep me happy. Those aren't necessarily the vendors you want. They just want to make their money back and they'll take anyone and charge anything to do it.

How to find your A Team:

Referrals. Referrals. REFERRALS. This is the best way to find your wedding vendors. This is where you can ask your friends and family for their advice rather than for their services. Think of a wedding you've been to and think about what you loved. Ask them who they used. You don't have to make every aspect of your wedding different from the last. Your friends won't call you a copy cat. They'll be flattered that you enjoyed their wedding enough to ask for recommendations. Sometimes these professionals are absolutely phenomenal but you just can't find them on Google. Not everyone has a huge budget to be able to get to page one or two of Google. That doesn't mean they're not amazing at what they do. People always make the mistake of going with the first company they find on the internet. Anyone can pay for advertizing. Anyone with a bit of money. Money doesn't buy talent. See Paris Hilton's music career.

Once you've locked down one under the radar vendor then it just gets easier from here. We wedding vendors love helping each other out. It's ugly out there and we rely on each other for that word of mouth to bring in our business. We need to work hard, we need to provide outstanding service and we need to promote our friends in the industry to compete with the big fish. We little fish charge less (because we don't have to make back those hefty advertizing costs) and we work ten times harder. We strive to create perfection because that's what people remember. That's what brings in repeat business. If the big fish screw up it's no sweat off their back because they have a hundred more clients lined up. That doesn't mean they produce shit. It just means they don't have to work as hard. We work harder and we're bloody passionate. And we have less clients on the go so you get more attention. Chances are that florist you hired; who you clicked with and had a great feeling about has a list of vendor friends that she'd recommend. They will be in the same price range and have the same personality and professionalism that made you fall in love with the first one. After all, you are who your friends are.

The next best way to find your wedding vendors is through your wedding planner. He or she has a shortlist of vendor friends she goes to for everything. I have about 10-15 vendors in each category. They're all different and unique (because no two weddings are the same), they're of different ranges on the price scale but their services are all one in the same. Outstanding. I've worked with them, I've built relationships with them and I trust them. They're reliable and they have the same work ethics as I do. Bonus for you, they offer me discounts that I pass on to you.

Let your wedding planner and your loved ones be your Google. It'll shave your budget and it will shave your stress.

6

It's the Little Things that Don't Count

INSIGNIFICANT DETAILS NOT WORTH STRESSING OVER

Do you have the kind of partner who will bring you breakfast in bed? Give you their last bite? Hold your hair back when you're heaving over the toilet after your best friend's bachelorette party? Have you come home only to find your eight year old doing to the dishes because she says she wants to help you? Does your BFF send you random texts saying how much she values and appreciates your friendship? All these little things count. I, for one, am a sucker for sweet nothings and love in all of its forms. I love the little things in life and truly believe we should all stop and smell the roses, so to speak. Take a second and really focus on the little things our near and dear ones do to put a smile on our faces. And it's equally important to press pause from work, school, meetings, washing, cleaning and stressing to show those we love what they mean to us and give them some loving back - even if it's in the smallest way imaginable. It counts and it gets noticed.

Here's what doesn't get noticed. What do not matter are the off-white David Austen roses in your centerpieces as opposed to the ivory ones. Do you think your guests are going to walk into the reception venue and the first thing they will say is, "Are you kidding me, she went with off-white? That was so four months ago." The majority of your guests have completely overlooked the décor and have already gone straight for the hors d'oeuvres or the antipasto table. The last thing they're thinking about are your arrangements. The room could be empty and believe me, they wouldn't notice. Yes, I know, you want them to walk in and say "Wow, she is just amazing, the collaboration between the David Austen roses, the peonies and the baby's breath really bring out the damask in the linens. What a brilliant choice!" Sorry ladies, unless your guest list comprises of David Tutera, Preston Bailey and Colin Cowie then I don't think you have anything to worry about.

I once had a bride who spent eight weeks emailing me every day with a HUGE dilemma. She could not decide on white linens with a textured table runner and some funky chargers or just a really cool stand out linen. Now I know this can be a pretty challenging decision for many people because if your guests are going to remember one thing it's going to be the linens! Was this chick for real? Now don't get me wrong, I'm a wedding planner. I live, breathe and dream weddings. I love them. I do think these decisions matter because after all, you're spending a hell of a lot of money on one day; you're going to want it to be pretty spectacular. Also, this day is special and you want it to be unique, trendy and all that jazz. I feel you. There is a happy medium between being bat shit crazy, which you may call "detail oriented" and just throwing your hands up in the air and saying you don't care.   .

For some reason, however, people take far too much time on linens. You do realize people eat on these? Kids throw food around, drunk guest spill their drinks, wax gets all over them from the hundreds of candles you have scattered all over them and not to mention these tables are so full of cutlery, crockery, forty glasses, menus, table numbers, and chances are a huge centerpiece that you can barely tell that there is a linen at all!

These details should be considered and decided upon in a pretty short amount of time. If you've only got six months from the ring to the end of the aisle then I suggest pick your battles and learn to budget your time a little more wisely. Moral of the story, go with white or any other simple colour that the venue offers and call it a day. If you want to add some flare then I suggest you throw some standout materials on the head table. That's it. Linens are not something you need to be outsourcing on a tight schedule or a tight budget.

I have an endless list of examples of brides (and grooms) that have spent their precious time obsessing over the wrong things. How about invites? This is one of my favourite topics. There are couples who spend two months obsessing over fonts and paper stock, and then there's Emily and Rory. I just got a pretty awesome invitation to their wedding. It was a 3D View-Master. If you didn't grow up in the 90's you have no idea what I'm talking about. It's one of those binocular like devices that have corresponding "reels" which are thin discs that have photos on them. Don't know what I'm talking about yet, I'll give you a minute to scan this barcode:

Scan BARCODE for the ViewMaster here:

This was one of the most creative invites I have ever seen in my life. This was something well worth spending over $10 per invite for two reasons. One: it's not going in the garbage. Your guests won't do the typical glance and skim through for the date and then toss it in the drawer until it gets closer. Two: it can be used again and again! For your thank you cards, Christmas cards and any other cards, just send your friends and family another reel for them to insert into the View-Master. Brilliant. Of course, you need to tell them your plan or sadly, it may go in the garbage. Nonetheless, this invite is memorable. It's a conversation starter. I compare every invite I get to this one now. This couple had a smallish guest list and not a lot of time to put their wedding together, after all they have two kids and they both work full time. They still managed to pull off a cute and creative invitation to announce their nuptials.

Then you have the crazies. I do not use this word lightly. Another past client of mine was a complete nightmare when creating her invitations. She chose to do them herself. I have a little advice on DIY: don't do it. It's a headache. It's not worth it and you'll see why. Let me take you on a walk down memory lane. First it was the paper. We went to every paper shop in the city and the options available to her were just not good enough. She had 18 months to plan her wedding. This is what happens when you have far too much time. And when you're certifiably insane. After the paper it was the font. She happened to like my handwriting and wanted me to handwrite their names at the top of the invite as a logo. Don't even get me started. The amount of times I had to write their names practically gave me carpal tunnel syndrome. She liked this stroke better than that one and could I draw the last letter on the first sample the way I drew it on the eighth sample, but a little less flick like the one on the twelfth sample. Dealing with behaviours like this is what drives people to drink. When the font was decided on a few weeks later, then we were on to the colour. Was it going to be Pantone Bluebonnet or Blueberry? The differences in the colour swatches she was showing me were so miniscule and on the paper she selected they literally looked exactly the same when they were printed. This is when I began to twitch because I couldn't take it anymore. It was completely ludicrous. I had asked her if this was really that big of a decision and she could have cut right through me with the daggers she glared at me with. Ok, guess not then. When all was finally decided on about four weeks and 37 samples later, we had to find a matching blue ribbon bellyband and burlap rope to be wrapped around it. This was exceptionally fun because as her bridesmaids and I started putting them together - cutting the exact measurements she asked for and wrapping them around the invite - she would check every single one, take it apart and rearrange it so it was not even one tenth of a millimeter off of her specifications. Once everything was wrapped and approved she went on the hunt for the perfect rustic brown paper bag envelopes to put her creation in and send them off to her friends and family. The whole process took her six weeks. SIX weeks! To put invites together and send them off. Online paper shops do this in 48 hours. And just to put it into perspective, these could have been ordered and packaged for around $7 per full invite. This seemed too much for my bride so she did everything in parts.

Here's the breakdown:

	DIY	Professional
Paper	$ 200.00	
Belly Bands	$ 100.00	
Envelopes	$ 100.00	
Printer Cartridges	$ 200.00	
Guillotine Cutter	$ 50.00	
Labels	$ 100.00	
Postage	$ 65.00	$ 65.00
Time	PRICELESS	
TOTALS	$ 815.00	$ 765.00
Single invite cost based on 100	$ 8.15	$ 7.65

You literally pay more when you do them yourself. You just don't notice because you're paying little by little and don't keep track of all the payments. Scratch the DIY and save yourself the headache. Seriously people, pick your battles. I'm not going to lie to you, these invites were beautiful. Were they worth the time and stress to put them all together? Absolutely not. After asking a few of her friends what they thought of her invites they had said they didn't even remember what they looked like or where they had put them. What day was it on again? Luckily I wasn't there for that conversation. The vein in the centre of her forehead was probably ready to burst.

Sorry I spent three seconds reviewing the wedding invitation you spent three months on.

som**ee**cards

I know it's hard not to get wrapped up in little details that you think make a world of a difference in your special day. It's really hard not to imagine that your guests will be talking about these details for many years to come and every wedding they go to after yours just won't quite live up to it because yours was so thought out and your colours were perfect, and you were just so meticulous and brilliant. I'm sorry dears, reality check: They will not. Your guests will remember a couple of very important things. The food, the party and the drinks. The rest of the details will just fade away as time goes on and your wedding becomes older news than Jay-Z and Solange's elevator fight. All you're left with are some pictures and hopefully your husband.

Since we're telling horror stories, here's another one. Another one of my lovely brides (and this is not sarcasm, they were all lovely, weddings just do something crazy to people!) was dead set on flowerless centerpieces. Bare birch branches with hanging tea light candles. They went perfectly with her rustic venue. Well, this bride didn't have the budget for them so she too decided to enter the wonderful world of DIY. After six months of battling with these centerpieces, believe me - that world was not so wonderful anymore. Putting the branches together was a piece of cake. If all you have to do is throw a few branches in a tall vase then DIY your little heart out. This was a bit more complicated than that. This is where the fun part really kicked in. The candles. I'm going to be very specific here so you can understand what lengths this chick went to, to put these things together. First she had to poke a teeny little hole in on either side of the candle casing to feed fish wire through and then tie up the ends and hang it on the branches. When she made an example one to show to her bridal party she said it only took her about 10 minutes from start to finish. First of all this was an outright lie. Have you ever handled fishing wire? It's completely impossible and unless you're the Crocodile Dundee then you can just forget it. She then went on to explain that each centerpiece needed at least 15 hanging candles so it wouldn't look empty. If you're not good at math, that's a minimum of 150 minutes per centerpiece. I'm sure you're wondering how many centerpieces there were? There were 30. With some more adding, multiplying and dividing you'll work out that that's 75 hours on centerpieces. Do you know what you can do with 75 hours? My job pays me a pretty decent salary for that many hours work. What did these girls get? Blisters. They also got a micro manager, who over the next few weeks of a couple hours here and there (another lie), would breathe down their necks making them tie and untie the candles so they were at a height that was to her liking. And we're talking millimeters here. They had to look "scattered". I'm sure you get the point. Now, if this lovely bride had filled me in on her illegal sweatshop that she was running in the comfort of her own basement I would have asked her if she tested one before going into overdrive. Did she light one and hang it for say six hours to see what happened? Well she hadn't. Not only were the little elves frantically working the night before the wedding when they should have been watching Bridesmaids and getting tipsy, on the day of the wedding can you guess what happened? During dinner people were enjoying hot wax with their meals as candles came crashing down. In about 60 seconds flat, 75 hours of slavery went out the window as all the candles were blown out and taken away by panicked catering staff. This not only gave the bride crazy eyes on her wedding day but it disrupted the whole wedding, not to mention, nearly poisoned her guests. Do you think anyone would have noticed if those gorgeous bare birch branches were left bare? I wouldn't have. People never notice what's not there. Not one person would have walked in and said "Those are beautiful but something's missing, I think its scattered hanging tea light candles." She would have gotten the same feel if she scattered them around the vase on the table.

Point being lovelies, whether you're marrying in six months or six weeks, don't DIY if it's overly complicated. Even if it seems simple, it's not. Just don't do it. Those 75 hours her friends and family spent cursing her under their breath and rolling their eyes could have been replaced with $30 per centerpiece and a whole lot of time for margaritas and BFF bonding. That's what your bridal party is for. Plus, what the fuck are you going to do with all the crap you put together after the wedding? Sell it? No one will buy it. Apparently hoarding is a thing. Don't let it be your thing. Avoid this by renting your decor and calling it a day. Creative professionals will do a much better job of putting pretty things together.

Ask any bride who's just tied the knot. Ask her if the ribbon she used to tie her favour bags - which took her eight weeks to find - made any difference at all in the grand scheme of her wedding day. She'd probably roll her eyes and say that it made zero impact. We find ourselves obsessing over the tiniest of things and guess what? No one notices.

Here are some details that everyone will tell you are essential and that I beg to differ about:

Lighting: This is where DJ and/or entertainment companies make the bulk of their money. They'll walk into a beautiful venue and want to change everything up. Yes some venues need an up-light or two to give it a bit of a lift. But, let's not forget, these venues were built with perfectly acceptable complimenting lighting. It's not like this is a factor they overlooked when the venue was being built. They weren't like: "Nah, we don't need lighting in here, can't be bothered. We'll just have outside companies come in and do it for us." When planning our wedding, we completely overlooked lighting. I saw what the room looked like with just what the venue had to offer and I was fine with it. Would a splash of pink and purple make it look cool? Sure. Would people notice? Maybe. Would they feel like something was missing if we just dimmed the lights and put a couple of up lights along the wall of the head table? Nope. No one said, "Wow, this would be way more beautiful if they brought in four chandeliers." We spent $100 on four up-lights we rented from Long and McQuade and put them along the head table. When it does matter: If you're getting married outside. Clearly you don't want to be in darkness. Solution: Fairy lights. Boom.

Decor: Things get noticed if they're there, but they don't get noticed if they're not. This may sound repetitive, but this one piece of advice needs to be drummed into your pretty little heads. In the five months I had to plan my wedding would you believe I completely forgot to consider any sort of decor for my head table? You know the fun of pipe and draping. I had about fourteen thousand things on my mind and when I was sitting down with my wedding planner and we were talking about the head table, I may have thought about it for a brief second but I just said, "Look, let's keep it simple with a lot of candles and lanterns - no flowers and just a simple long table with white linen. Nothing major." If I had more time on my hands I would have thought, "Ok, let me go home and think about this." Off to the blogs I would have gone and I would have come back with too many Pinterest ideas worth about $5000. I'm glad I didn't. If I had the budget for it I would have given that number to my coordinator and said "Go nuts!" But I didn't. Remember my flower theory. If you've got the budget for the flowers and you can Kimye the crap out of the room then absolutely, people will notice. If you don't - like I didn't - then people won't notice anything's missing. It's really simple. I didn't bring in a vinyl dance floor and no one pointed out the fact that it wasn't there. If I had, it would have looked cool, sure. Then everyone would be over it in one hot minute. That's what you're paying for when you're fiddling with all these details. That first impression your guests have. I'm not saying don't do it. As long as it's within your means. On a budget and looking for places to cut costs? That's where I'd start. Besides, you should be considering these things right from the get go. If you know you have a tiny decor budget then pick a place that doesn't require much. Obviously, if you get married in a greenhouse on a farm that barely comes with tables and chairs then be prepared to dish out the majority of your budget on filling it up. If you can't - then don't even go there.

The bathrooms: This boggles my mind a bit when I do site visits and the bride says, "Oh I have to see the bathroom - we need to see how many flowers we need to order for them." Um, in the bathroom? The bathroom's where guests are doing their business, sometimes guests are throwing up in (sadly yes - there's always one) or where they're in for two minutes re-applying their makeup and rushing back to the party. Why the hell would you even consider decorating them? If you're having an outdoor wedding I highly recommend renting some Porta-potties, whether they're standard or luxurious, because if you didn't that would definitely get noticed. Your guests not having a place to release the fluids they've been consuming may pose as a problem - but that is about as far as I would go when considering toilets. Just make sure they're there. The rest is ridiculous.

I could never forget the anniversary of me ruining your wedding.

someecards

A second dress: I don't get this. Why do you need another one? How greedy are you? It's not an award show and you're not Giuliana Rancic hosting Miss Universe where you are required a wardrobe change after every commercial so designers can showcase their work. And do you know how long it takes to change? I didn't go to the bathroom because I didn't want to miss a beat - changing into an entirely new dress would take at least half an hour. No thanks. Again, at around midnight no one is on the edge of their seat (you'd hope they'd be on the dance floor) wondering when you're coming out in dress number two and who you'll be wearing. Seriously. If you want a bit of a change, here's what I just suggested to a friend of mine who is getting married next fall. She could not decide for the life of her between a strapless dress or a dress with three quarter lace sleeves. I recommended she get a strapless gown that can be added to. All she would need is the dressmaker to make her a simple French lace jacket that would go over her shoulders and completely mesh with the material of the dress to make it look like a long sleeve gown. She could wear that to the church ceremony and then take it off for the party. This option has a lot of plusses. One, she saves money on a second dress. French lace overlay would only cost a couple of hundred dollars. Second, she would have two completely different looks with one dress and she'd have a nice variety of photos. Lastly, long sleeve dresses are great, but they can get very hot when you're partying it up on the dance floor. Having a removable jacket is super convenient because when you get too hot you can just take it off. Not the case with a long sleeve gown.

The exit: A lot of people stress about making this memorable exit. They plan the song, a little skit or exit they think will go down in history. By the time you're ready to leave most people are already gone and the ones that are still there are too busy taking advantage of last call to even notice you're gone. Spend the last few moments taking everything in. The night is almost over and this is it. Grab your new hubby, cheers to the night and just look around at all the people that are having an awesome time celebrating the beginning of the rest of your life. I did it. I tell all my brides to do it. And I strongly recommend it. I took a mental picture, I stopped to think about how happy I was at that very moment and I will have that memory forever. It was pretty fucking amazing.

All the other stuff: Centerpieces, invites, place cards, napkins, menus, favours, cutlery, linens...the list is endless. Yes, have them. Make them cute but don't sweat it so much. They'll be seen, they'll be used and they'll be taken home, maybe thrown in a drawer or the garbage, but they won't be remembered. I got an invite from someone and it was etched into wood. No, I'm not kidding. First of all, you can't put it on the fridge because it's too damn heavy and secondly, it's so stupid. Do you think I looked at it and said, "Wow these people are rich, I envy them"? No. I thought to myself, "wow, why didn't I think of this brilliant idea that brides will eat up?" Sorry if you've done it and I've offended you, and PS you may be reading the wrong book, but I can think of a million other things to spend my money on than an invitation heavier than my iPad. I'd rather send an e-vite and give the money I saved to charity.

I'm not saying that everything is a waste of money. I just think it's insane when people go too far.

People go by the latest trends and not what really reflects them. It's not like I didn't have place cards. Of course I did. And they were adorable. It was a little typewriter ($0.30 each at Creative Bag) and in it sat the person's name and a little note: "Thank you for travelling 10,687 kms to be here with us" I did this for two reasons: First, I didn't have 600 people at my wedding so I didn't have to calculate the distance that many people travelled and more importantly because I wanted my guests (particularly my Aussie ones and the ones that travelled far) to know I appreciated their efforts. This is when shit makes a difference. It's when you're including your guests in the details, something like that touches them. I took the time to individually thank them again in a different way. These place cards - so small and insignificant - were also conversation starters. Everyone was interested to see how far everyone came. And I incorporated them into the centerpiece giveaway because whoever travelled the furthest got to take the centerpiece home. I made a tiny detail about them and not me. When you show people they're special and important to you then they'll take notice. Yes, they'll notice the hanging florals and be impressed by the hanging wedding cake for a few seconds, but there isn't an emotional connection there so as fast as they take notice is as fast as they'll forget. I still see my place cards in friends' homes when we go over for dinner. I see the centerpieces as part of their decor. That's the stuff that people remember.

There's one thing that your guests will notice if you don't do. Thank you cards. IMPORTANT. Petite detail that you think no one will remember after the wedding. Besides, you gave them a favour and your wedding is ancient history. Right? Wrong. They're all waiting for one. It makes me crazy when couples say, "I just haven't had time to do my thank you cards". I'm sorry, you had time to take a year out of your life to plan your inordinate wedding but you don't have a couple of hours to send the people you asked to share it with you a token of your appreciation? No, sorry, I don't buy it. It's infuriating. How dare you consume yourself and everyone else for months, inconvenience people's lives AND accept gifts from all of them and not send them a thank you? Or even worse, take 6 months to get them out only for them to find a generic one liner basically saying 'thanks for the gift but I couldn't be bothered thinking of anything personal to say so I paid Wedding Paper Divas to do it for me.'

Online paper shops will send out a beautiful thank you card and you can get it blank on the back so you can write a PERSONALIZED message to each guest. Which I strongly advise. Cut the "I don't have time" bullshit because you do have time. Take a day off, just like you took several leading up to your wedding. If you don't want to write out 500 messages then you shouldn't have accepted 500 people's gifts. Common courtesy has gone out the window and it needs to come back. This to me is bad taste if it's done any other way. I'm not fussed if you're offended, if you take this book straight to the garbage after reading this sentence. These people bent over backwards for you. Take a weekend, grab your new husband and a bottle of wine (a few bottles depending on the size of your guest list) and get your best penmanship out. Time to start saying thanks.

7

Competition

DO IT FOR YOU…NOT FOR THOSE YOU
WANT TO IMPRESS

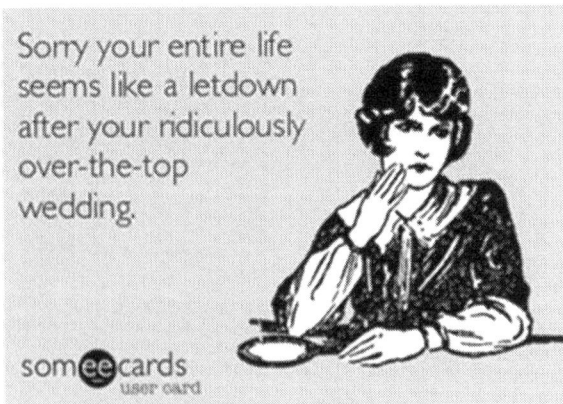

Sorry your entire life seems like a letdown after your ridiculously over-the-top wedding.

someecards
user card

Ladies, please listen carefully. This is the number one reason why wedding budgets get blown out of proportion. It's the same factor that drives you to save all your pennies - or rack up all your credit cards - to buy that Prada handbag that tells everyone you are in fact better than them. When the reality is, you're one more late payment away from your hot water being cut off. But it's all worth it when you look over to the girl standing next to you and she's looking at you and your Prada in admiration, right? How shallow are you?

I have a theory, and that's if you can afford it, get it; if you can't, keep walking. I love fashion. I too, can be quite the label whore, but I don't let competition and envy control my bank account. If there's something I really want and I don't have to sacrifice lunch for a month then I'll get it. After all, what's the point of working so hard if you can't treat yourself to something pretty? It doesn't matter if it's an overpriced evening bag, a piece of contemporary art for your dining room or an overpriced luxe cake on your wedding day. None of these things are necessities, but if it's within your means, and most importantly if it's because you love it and not because you need to show it off, then go nuts. Who am I to tell you what I think is worth it and what isn't? I spent $200 on a six foot giraffe for my baby's nursery. Most people would say I'm a total moron. I'm not being a hypocrite because this isn't me telling you what you should and shouldn't buy, or what is or isn't worth it. This isn't about that. This is about making decisions within your wedding budget comfortably FOR YOU.

Say, for instance, you have a $1000 budget for your dress and shoes. This to some is a lot of money on an outfit you're only going to wear once. To others, it doesn't even scrape the surface because that budget will not get you your Monique Lhuillier dress and the perfect Louboutin's. You can try searching far and wide for sample sales and hey, you may get lucky. But realistically, you won't. With a short engagement and a smaller budget, you don't have time to run around frantically looking for the best labels, at the best prices, in the perfect sizes. You have a couple of options, but walking down the aisle in couture labels is not one of them. Does it really matter, though? There are thousands and thousands of boutiques who carry independent designer dresses. These dresses are gorgeous, they're affordable and they're unique. Just because they don't have 1.3m followers on Instagram doesn't mean they're any less talented. And your dress isn't a handbag. It doesn't have the label plastered across the front for your guests to drool over. Not that it matters.

Choose a budget that you can afford and stick to it. If that budget allows you to get Vera Wang herself design you a custom made dress then call her up. If it only allows you to head to David's Bridal and go for a less exclusive label then this should make you just as happy. It's not about the name. It's about feeling beautiful and confident in something you're going to be wearing on one of the happiest day of your life. It's about walking down that aisle and dancing the night away in something that reflects your personal style. What's the point of draining your savings just to get the latest trend from the Oscar de la Renta 2015 collection if you feel like a complete asshole in it? All eyes are on you, remember. Cameras are in your face and everyone's watching. If you feel like what you're wearing doesn't belong on you then chances are people can see that. You don't want everlasting photos showing an awkward, uncomfortable bride on her wedding day. Just because a dress you love looked flawless on the model that was specifically chosen to strut her stuff in it at NY Bridal Fashion Week, does not mean that if you drop $10,000 that it will look just as good on you.

I once had a bride who hired me for full wedding coordination. Let's call her Allie. After getting to know my couples, the first thing I ask is "what's your budget?" Allie gave me a budget of $40,000. Perfect, I thought. Totally reasonable and achievable, we could plan the wedding of her dreams within that magic number. We chatted over coffee - about their loves and hates, about what they wanted their wedding reception to reflect to their guests and what they wanted to remember most when they looked back at their wedding. The answers were sensible and down to earth. They always are, at first. She said she wanted her guests to get a sense of who they were when they walked in. She wanted the theme of the wedding to paint a picture of their love story. She went on to tell me that she wanted to look back and remember a stress-free day that was simple and fun. She wanted great food and an awesome atmosphere and guests to walk away saying, "That was the best wedding EVER!"

As the months passed - 22 months to be exact - Allie went from being laid back and down to earth to a straight up wannabe Kardashian. She wanted the best of everything. My number one job as her wedding planner was to get her what she wanted within her budget. Despite my efforts to keep her grounded, by the time the big day rolled around her budget had tripled to a whopping $120,000. I wish I was exaggerating. Over those 22 months she over educated herself with all the latest wedding news. If she applied half the effort into something like her job or a charity she probably could have changed the world. I'm aware that that's something my mother would say, but it's true. She took notes at every wedding she had gone to, snapped some mental shots and put them in her pocket so when her day came she could one up them all. She learned who was who in the wedding world and where did she start? Wedluxe. Wedluxe is an online wedding blog that features the most exclusive real brides of Canada. These blogs are also where I spend the majority of my research time. These weddings are tasteful, they are flawless, and as you can possibly guess, outrageously expensive.

Scrolling through all these pages can give you some gorgeous wedding ideas, but it can also turn you into a really ugly person who is raging green with envy. The more you research, the more you want your wedding to be featured on this site. The envy begins. You've seen enough, your mind is made up, you skim through the photos until you get to 'the List'.

The List is amazing for wedding vendors and suppliers such as myself. If you're on the List then you're in high demand. These brides don't care who you are or what else you've done. You're what they want because you put them one step closer to showing everyone they are amazing. It's pretty ridiculous. We as wedding vendors also work incredibly hard to get on Wedluxe just to be a part of the List. All you need is one wedding. One bride who wants to be featured and is willing to go the distance to make that happen and if you're lucky enough to be involved in her wedding and it gets featured, you scroll down and see Wedding Planning by BeLaV on that exclusive List and you're set. It's the Holy Grail of wedding planning.

As you scroll through these stunning photos you see the names Chanel, Tiffany's, Lazaro, Rolex, and Louboutin, to name a few, and you get a little star struck. I totally get that. But, you have to stay grounded and realistic. Just because some girl you don't know is showing off her Jimmy Choos, doesn't mean you need to get all huffy and puffy because all you can afford are a pair of Zara pumps. Unless you're sporting a mini, no one is going to see them anyway. Oh, but you're planning on getting your photographer to take a photo of them so you can post it on Facebook, right? If you're dropping the cash just to show them off in one way or another then I suggest you get your priorities straight. Why is it so important? You're about to marry the love of your life but you're having a hissy fit over a pair of shoes that you can't afford. If you're getting so upset over a pair of shoes maybe you need to ask yourself what you're really upset about. Don't be an asshole. We all desire pretty and expensive things. All these designers are really good at making us think we NEED them to be happy. We NEED them for our day to be perfect. We NEED them to seal our happily ever after. It's called marketing, everyone.

Since we're on the topic of competition, let's talk about ring envy. This doesn't start from the day you get engaged, it starts the day you realize this guy is your forever. From that day on when you talk to other women the first thing you do is look down. If they're rocking one then you're no longer listening to what they're saying you're just taking mental pictures and putting them in your library. When you get yours it's going to be SO much better. Then once you've got it you're still on the hunt. Scoping out everyone's hands making sure yours is better than everyone else's. A few years down track these little bitches you see are walking around with 3 carats. That's the norm now so you're looking for an upgrade because your 1 carat is pathetic in comparison. Let's rewind for a moment and I'll give you a little history lesson.

From the American Gem Society:

In the 1930s, when demand for diamond rings declined in the U.S. during hard economic times, the De Beers Company began an aggressive marketing campaign using photographs of glamorous movie stars swathed in diamonds. Within three years, the sales of diamonds had increased by 50 percent. In 1947, De Beers launched its now classic slogan, "A Diamond is Forever." This spurred even more sales. The implied durability of a diamond conveyed the meaning in the American psyche that marriage is forever. A diamond's purity and sparkle have now become symbols of the depth of a man's commitment to the woman he loves in practically all corners of the world.

See the full story here!

Yes, you read right. It's all a marketing ploy to take your hard earned moolah. And before you go googling me and calling me a total fraud - yes I do have a diamond engagement ring. Who doesn't love diamonds? There's nothing wrong with that. Regardless of where it came from, everyone is excited to get the ring. That's not my concern. The reasons WHY are my focus. Chicks go nuts over size. They can't wait to get this rock so they can show off how big it is. That's their main concern.

"Make sure you get me a 2ct because my ring has to be bigger than Denise's ring."

"Alexis barely has a carat - ew. You can barely see it"

"OMG is her ring bigger than mine? Day – RUINED!"

"Doesn't Emily's ring look like it came out of a gumball machine? Pathetic."

Talk like this makes me sick to my stomach. I knew of a girl who would not allow her now EX-husband to propose unless he proposed with a 2ct Tiffany's diamond. If it was anything less she wasn't interested. Then she'd give him shit because he was taking too long to pop the question. How they even made it to the altar was beyond me - but they didn't get very far. How many of you were given the opportunity to choose or design your own ring? How many of you can tell me that your friends rings had no influence on your decision? I know at least half of you are lying to me and to yourselves. Not just as women, but as human beings we get wrapped up in competition. We put all this pressure on our partners to save and work over time and dump three months' salary into something we wear on our finger. Something that by the time we have kids, and are married for a while, our hands are usually covered in food, shit, soil, manure; we barely wear the ring anymore so we don't lose or ruin it. Do you know that the difference between one and two carats is millimeters? But the price difference is thousands. Even going from a .9ct ring to a 1.0ct ring is a couple thousand dollars. Smarten up ladies. That's a trip to Fiji.

If your soon to be fiancé is struggling or isn't a millionaire, don't put that kind of pressure on him for the sake of having a sparklier hand than your friend. Rings and diamonds are beautiful, but that's all. They are not the symbol of the man's love for you. They are purely a status symbol and you're not Jennifer Aniston. Quit whining and don't make it something it's not. I'm starting to sound like a broken record, but I can't stress enough that if you can, great, if you can't, who cares. It's just stuff. Stuff that's not worth getting bent out of shape over. Just because you're not sporting a rock doesn't mean shit. I couldn't care less what the girls around me are wearing. I'm a bit more concerned about my marriage. Or the trips we plan on going on, or the dinners we plan on going out for, or a hundred other things that turn into memories that are far more precious than diamonds. Don't get me wrong, I love them. And I love my ring. It's modest and it's gorgeous. It represents a lot more than a dollar figure. I wouldn't change a thing. I love it because it's mine, it's from him and that has nothing to do with anyone else. I'm always looking at people's rings, I'm just not swooning over them. I come across so many in my day to day life as a wedding planner. I don't have a pang of envy. I appreciate beautiful things, I'm just aware that I can't have everything and I simply do not care.

I was out with friends not long ago and I looked over to one of them and said, "Wow you're ring looks gorgeous, did you just get it cleaned?" You won't believe what she said. "I carry this jewelry cleaner around on me at all times. You never know when you'll need to give you're ring a shine to make people jealous." Really? Did she just say that? I was dumbfounded. How can someone be so insecure that she needs to hide behind a bit of bling? All that kind of attitude shows off are your insecurities. It's like ugly fat men driving around in flashy convertibles. I think we all know that means they have a small penis. Same goes for rings in my books. If you're going out of your way to flash it around, that's probably the only thing that you have left to be happy for. And that makes me feel sorry for you.

***

When I pay for a product or service, I want the best too. I want to make sure I'm paying for quality, especially when I'm dishing out a lot of money. Sites like Wedluxe and The Lane do only put up quality weddings that certainly have to meet a specific criteria, but that by no means implies that your wedding wasn't worthy if you didn't get featured. Allie wanted to be featured. She wanted it more than anything. She was acting like an insecure teenager who was just dying to fit in with the cool kids. She wanted her 15 minutes and she didn't care what it took. Why? Her best friend was getting married three months before her and she was going down the same path. The only difference was that her friend had a much larger budget that was being funded by her parents.

So what happened to Allie? Exactly what you'd imagine. She started feeling insecure when exchanging details with her BFF. She became driven by competition and all she wanted to do was "out-wedding her" Yeah, I said out-wedding. It's a thing. A very real thing. The entire feel of her wedding changed from simple and fun to over the top and very tense. Every discussion was based on, "Will this be Wedluxe worthy?" If the answer was no then more flowers were ordered, the centerpieces got bigger and every new trend was added which in turn inflated the budget. You're probably thinking that I didn't do a very good job at keeping within her budget, and you're right, I didn't. I'm a wedding planner, not a financial advisor. I can only advise to a certain point. If you can justify taking out a second mortgage to finance your decor and I tell you it's probably not a good idea but you insist, then I will get you the most beautiful flowers at the best possible price. I'm not interested in taking advantage of people. Not my thing. But, getting my clients what they want is also my job. Don't mistake this for magic. I'm pretty amazing at what I do, but I'm no Fairy Godmother either. I can get you a better price than you can get without a wedding planner, but I certainly can't fit $15,000 worth of flowers into a $40,000 budget. You want glamour beyond glamour then your budget needs to go up. Same goes with everything respectfully. Allie justified upping the budget with everything from the chargers to photographer who was willing to manipulate all their photos to meet the criteria and sign Wedluxe the rights to them. This, along with many other additions is how she went from $40,000 to $120,000.

What helped contribute to the rage that was the competition? All that time on her hands. 22 months to research her little heart out until she became a lunatic. Not once during this process did I hear anything about making the love of her life her husband. For nearly two years I didn't hear one thing about spending the rest of her life with the man of her dreams. I did hear, however, that he wasn't involved in the wedding plans and never helped with anything. He was always too busy working. Well, I wonder why? Someone has to finance all this nonsense. So the wedding came and went, it was featured on Wedluxe a short nine months later. Nine months later she was still paying off the one day that was now a distant memory. She had gone to three weddings since her own that were each said to be the best wedding EVER until the next one. But why weren't people saying, "This wedding is OK, but Allie's was so much better! Nothing will ever top that one!" Because no one remembered. And not to mention she was so focused on the materialistic things that she forgot to consider the element of fun. She used the venues on site DJ, she didn't have an MC to interact with her guests and help with the flow of the evening and she cheaped out on the food. Well, that my dears, is one thing that people remember. Going home hungry. If you can't afford to properly feed your guests maybe you should cut your decor costs and stop being selfish. Yes it's your day, but your guest deserve to be fed and fed well. They won't remember the chargers they were eating off of but they will remember their stomachs grumbling and leaving early to get a kebab before going home.

For you brides on a tight timeline, there's no time to even think about competition. You have just about enough time to sit down with your fiancé, work out the main details and get to booking. You may skim through a magazine or two but the options are so endless that you just end up putting the mags down and saying "Screw this, what do WE want to do?" "What do WE like?" That's what we did. We weren't interested in the latest trends or in who was doing what so we could one up them. We created a style that was ours and we actually had fun planning our wedding!

Competition is ugly and it just highlights a person's insecurities. You look like more of a fool putting on a one day "Me" show trying to one up everyone you know (and everyone you don't know) and then moving back into your parent's basement. You think the jokes on all your friends because your wedding was featured on Style Me Pretty as "Wedding of the Year"? Sorry, chick, jokes on you because you're pathetic. Take that ball and roll with it for a while.

Kudos to you if you're financially well off and you can afford a six figure wedding. I'm sure you couldn't care less about competition. If you've got it flaunt it, they say. That's not to rub it into everyone's faces but it's all relative. You work hard, play hard and reward yourself. If that's with an elaborate wedding then all the power to you. You're not doing it to literally "flaunt it". Chances are you believe you deserve it and you're doing it for you. This should be a bride's mentality no matter what point on the money scale she's on. Whether you're rich, poor, frugal or sensible, the mind set should be the same. Don't think about what people will say or what they'll think or what blog you'll impress, think about what you love and, above all, what you can afford. And think about what you want to remember when you look back on your day and stick to it. Trends will fade away faster than seasons change and as long as you stay true to who you are then you'll always remember your wedding and look back on your pictures as one you love and not one tacky expensive day.

8

Details: Keep them to Yourself

DON'T ADVERTISE EVERY SINGLE LITTLE WEDDING DETAIL

Do you have that friend who updates her Facebook status every seven seconds? One day she's having a destination wedding and she's #soexcited; the next day she's dreaming of a #Bohochic glorified backyard barbecue and the day after that she's putting up photos of her weekend away at Niagara on the Lake and she's found her #dreamwedding location.

No doubt your mind will change a thousand times in the span of 24 hours and that's ok. Not only are we human, we're women, we're allowed to change our minds. That's why we have return policies. Could you imagine the state of the retail world if everything was final sale? Well, thank God you don't have to. You also don't have to let everyone in on your thought process as you try and nail down your wedding theme. You're not a celebrity so why are you acting like you're talking to all your fans as if they're waiting by their phones for your status update? They're not your fans, they're your friends. Your friends that have lives too! Try asking them about their days every so often rather than blabbering on about yourself. It's highly irritating. Rather than getting the 50 likes and comments you were hoping for, you're getting eye rolling and shit talking behind your back. Sorry. #sorrynotsorry

I'm a big advocate of keeping those details to yourself. And not just because it makes you look like an attention seeking narcissist who has serious commitment issues. Also because the moment you start playing show and tell is the moment people believe they're entitled to have a say in your plans. You'll get everyone telling you what you should and shouldn't be doing. "I saw that photo you put up on Instagram, that hanging wedding cake is ridiculous." or "OMG you're thinking all white dresses? People are going to be wondering who the bride is! That's stupid."

Whether you want to get married in the Bahamas or have a cocktail reception on a rooftop overlooking the city, it's something you should decide with your fiancée and seek advice from a couple of close friends if you're stuck on a decision. You don't need a bunch of haters telling you what to do. Once you open the floodgates and start sharing your details, everyone becomes an expert. Skip that and hire a real expert because your friend that just got engaged is telling you not to do all white dresses because she secretly thinks it's an amazing idea and when her day rolls around she now wants to do it. Your cousin who told you the hanging centerpiece is stupid just broke up with her boyfriend and currently hates everything about weddings. Your mother who wants you to hire a Asian DJ and a live Asian pop band straight from Hong Kong for the entertainment wants the best for you yes, but she also wants everything her way because she knows best.

You don't want to be that girl that your friends are finding it very hard to be happy for. It sucks. After all, you're engaged, you're planning your wedding and you're going to be a Mrs. in no time. You want your besties to be genuinely happy for you. And trust me, they want to be happy for you. When you're going on and on and on and on, though they're finding it very difficult, it becomes draining to even hear you speak. The calls and texts become less frequent and then the excuses start. "Oh sorry, I think I'm going to be sick all week so I won't be available for shoe shopping." Meaning: "No I don't want to follow you around to every shoe shop in the city while you find every reason not to get every pair of shoes you try on because they're just not perfect enough. I have better things to do. Like stare at the wall for seven hours. That would be less painful and more productive."

You're probably thinking that I sound like I'm speaking from experience and I am. I have a friend, let's call her Nicole. Nicole changes her mind more frequently than I change my underwear. She also goes into some serious detail when she's sharing the nitty-gritty of her big day. It's draining. To my life and to my iPhone. In one conversation she goes in 12 different directions and at around the 40 minute mark I find myself stuck against the wall charging my phone because my battery is nearly dead. Remember the days even before cordless phones? Good old landlines with the coil cord that prevented you from walking around and doing a hundred other things while talking (or in my case listening) to whoever it was on the other end? You feel completely trapped. That's how I feel when I speak to her. It gives me serious anxiety. It's been six months and she has no idea what's going on in my life. She hasn't cared to ask. The phone rings, I roll my eyes I pick it up and secretly wish that today she's calling to tell me something else. Anything else. Or better yet, she's calling to see how I am. Nope, she's calling to tell me that plans have changed and she's now getting married in Thailand. I try and be happy for her, I really, really try and I really want to be. But I've got nothing. I'm dead inside. She's made me stone cold. She's made the wedding planner not give two shits about a wedding. That takes some serious talent. You, my friends, do not want to be Nicole.

Turning into Nicole can be avoided. And it's really simple. All you have to do is get your head out of your ass and remember that your friends and family have lives and if you take notice it won't mean your wedding will be forgotten. It means while you're doing your thing, they're still doing theirs and it's your job as a friend to take notice.

I have another friend, I'm going to name her Sonya. What a breath of fresh air when she was getting married. We've been friends for quite a while and have lived across the street to across the ocean from each other. Along the way we both got engaged, got married, she's popped out a little munchkin and now I have one brewing. During her engagement year I was going through a bit of a tough time. Every single day she would call me and ask me how I was doing as if she didn't have a wedding three months away. This didn't only lift my spirits but it gave me the chance to ask her about her details. I was excited to hear about everything from the flowers to the photo booth. I couldn't get enough of her details and she couldn't get enough of my day to day updates. Since then, we've both had ups and downs in our lives and no one's "situation" was more important than the others. That's a friendship.

How about the element of surprise? One of my brides literally shared every single detail with

EVERYONE. She started with a countdown the moment she got engaged. And that was updated every single day for the next 452 days. True story. Who the hell are you talking to and what makes you think that your audience really gives a shit how many days to go before you tie the knot? Chances are you're barely inviting half of those people so why do you feel you need to constantly remind them of that fact? There are apps for these things. Download one and don't share it on anything. Coupled with the countdown, she'd add a line or two of where she was at with the wedding details. So not only could she remind people when the wedding was in case they forgot, they knew exactly what she was doing at all times. She even went as far as posting pictures of her dress fittings on Facebook. Like, hello? Do you want anything to be a surprise? Yes, I get that it's an old tradition to keep your dress a secret but don't you want to have a bit of a wow factor when you're in sight and are about to walk down the aisle? I know I sure did.

She (I) had some pretty awesome ideas that she just couldn't wait to share with anyone. I guess she had to let it out somehow. Solution: Don't have a century long engagement! Sure, you're going to want to share all your fun details with everyone and when the wedding is ages away you have the itch to buy and tell. But please ladies, listen to me. Everyone loves the element of surprise. If you want there to be positive buzz around your wedding then zip it and have people guessing right up until show time. The anticipation leading up to it will make your guests excited about the whole thing. If I knew every last detail down to the dress and shoes I wouldn't think I was going to anything special. There would be no gasp when the bride walks down the aisle because I've not only seen the dress I've seen the selfie she posted of the make-up and hair trial. I'd probably be refreshing my Instagram feed. Yawn.

At the beginning stages of our engagements we're more in love than ever, we're excited and our minds are racing in a thousand different directions. It's so easy to get caught up in the emotion of all things wedding related. Couples get so wrapped up in every single little detail and they lose complete sight of themselves and the real reason behind why they're getting married to begin with! I feel you, it's an electrifying time and you're over the moon. But you need to keep in mind that no one is going to forget you're getting married. You don't need to constantly bring it up. If you just shut the fuck up for five minutes and give everyone a chance to talk about themselves for a while then they will, without a doubt, ask you how your planning is coming along. And they're going to look forward to hearing it and above all, they'll like you a whole lot more. Trust me. Keep all the in-between crap to yourself and don't share until someone asks and you have deposits in place. That way you'll still have friends to talk to about everything with.

9

Time to Let Go of Miss Perfect

HOW TO GET A GRIP AND STOP BEING A CONTROL FREAK

"A jack of all trades is a master at none"
Anonymous

I know what you're thinking. "I know best and only I know what will work for MY wedding." I'm sure you do, darling. But it's time to release your inner control freak and start trusting other people to do what you hired them for. You're not a florist, a wedding planner, a graphic designer or a Food and Beverage Manager. Well, you might be, but I'm certain you're only one of those things. You can't

91

possibly be everything. You have a job, you have a wonderful family, you have friends and you have a lovely fiancée. You want to keep them all I'd imagine, so it's time to let go of the pointer and let the pros take over.

The worst thing anyone can do is tell someone how to do their job. Why hire them if you're going to breathe down their necks and not let them do what you're paying them to do? You probably researched to the end of the world and back for the best of the best so why aren't you confident in your choice? You call it constructive criticism. I call it being a control freak.

Letting go of your inner Little Miss Perfect, if you can even admit that you have this issue, may sound easy. But it can be quite hard to grasp for a lot of Bridezillas. For a very short time period I had a Bridezilla who would call me every ten minutes to check up on me. She second guessed every decision she had asked me to make and she went as far as calling all the vendors I made contact with to make sure I had ordered what she wanted correctly. I'm not a quitter, so I saw out our contract and stayed with her until 9:00 pm on the wedding day. I usually get invited to stay on for a drink but in this case there was no invitation and no regret on my part. I could not get out of there fast enough. On the day of the wedding she was too busy delegating to have a good time, let alone to acknowledge my existence.

You don't want to be that girl do you? You need to cool it. If you want to do something perfectly, then work on being perfectly imperfect. I'm sure you'd be great at anything you do but start embracing other people's opinions and start having faith that the world isn't comprised of useless incompetent human beings. Some of us actually know what we're doing. We've been doing it for a very long time and you may not believe this, but we do it better than you think you can. You don't have to give me every single worst case scenario of what can go wrong. As a wedding planner, believe me I've seen them all. I have contingency plans that you have never thought of so just take the back seat and enjoy the ride.

Here are a few ideas to help you let go of your inner (control) freak:

Acknowledgement

What's the first step of changing and letting go? Acknowledging that you have to change in the first place. Look your persona in the eyes, thank her for being there for you all those years and for all the good she's done for you, acknowledge all the bad, tell her you forgive her and finally cut the cord.

Don't set yourself up for disappointment

Reality Check: You can't control the weather. If you know that rain on your wedding day will put a damper on things - pun intended - then don't pick an outdoor venue. Foolproof, right? Wrong. You'll be so set on that venue with the outdoor garden and you'll say, "What are the chances?" The big day arrives and it's pouring. If you're not the type to throw on some rain boots and turn this negative into a positive then just avoid it all together.

Have realistic expectations

Take your dress for example. If you've hired a seamstress or a designer you need to have an open mind. Firstly, do not bring a picture of a dress you want replicated. This isn't only an insult to your dressmaker, it's downright unrealistic. A designer WILL NOT replicate someone else's dress and pass it off as their own. It's like the biggest faux pas in the fashion world. If you can't afford the Carolina Hererra one then expect the one your dressmaker is designing to be unique. If you don't accept this then you'll be disappointed with the final outcome. This is your wedding dress, you need to feel 100% happy and comfortable in it.

Let people do things their way for a change

I know you think your way is better. Or more efficient. Your way isn't necessarily the best way. There are factors to be considered in every job that you couldn't possibly think of. If you let someone else take the lead, someone who knows a thing or two about their profession, you can avoid major crises. For example, one of my brides wanted ghost chairs brought in for the ceremony and then moved to the dining room for the reception on the second floor. She just assumed the venue would be OK with this. She went ahead and ordered the chairs and paid a non-refundable deposit without asking me or the venue for advice. The venue came back saying that because it was a historical building, they did not allow outside rentals in the building. This was also in the contract that she had signed without letting me give it a once over. I always read through my clients contracts thoroughly, which is why I always ask to be present in all meetings. There are things in the fine print that you will miss if you're not looking for them. Trust us, we've done this before. I could have saved that girl a ton of money if she had just asked.

Have a wedding-free day

Once a week, at least. No wedding talk. No books. No mags. No blogs or anything wedding related. Yes, you don't have a year and a half to plan the big day, but one day a week will not kill you. Nor will it make all your wedding plans come crashing down. The world will continue to function believe it or not. We have weekends off work - well some of us do. It's for a reason. So we don't become delusional. Take some time here and there, let go of that authority and do something else. Otherwise, when the day comes and goes you'll be facing some serious post wedding withdrawals because you won't remember who you were or what you did with your time before you were engaged.

When the craving creeps up, channel your energy to your to do list

The one list you can have full control over and micro manage the shit out of. This is YOUR list of things to do. Your tasks, your job. When you feel the urge to check up on your suppliers or your friends and fam to ensure they're doing what you asked correctly and efficiently, just take a little walk over to the fridge and see what you can cross off your list and get to it.

Accept it's OK if everything isn't perfect

This makes a huge difference on your wedding day. The faster you can accept that things won't be 100% perfect, the more enjoyable your day will be. After a long ass day, your flowers will be a bit wilted, your dress will very likely be ripped or dirty by the time you're being introduced as Mrs. Charming, and the gorgeous fondant flower on your cake may have fallen off because it was 40 degrees that day. Yes, all that happened to me. I also bought a $100 pen that I wanted to sign the marriage license with which I forgot to use. Did I care about any of it? No. Because a thousand other things went right and I was literally floating on a cloud all day. Dealing with hundreds of weddings I know things ALWAYS go wrong. You don't have to be a wedding planner to have such a carefree attitude. You just have to be realistic and prepared. Just because things aren't perfect doesn't mean they can't be perfectly imperfect.

Listen. Think. Listen. Then speak.

When people talk are you too busy already reciting what you're going to say in your head? So the second they finish speaking you've already gone on a tangent? How's that working out for you? Try LISTENING. When you're too busy trying to think of a rebuttal your brain doesn't have enough room to actually listen to what the other person is saying. How can you tell someone they're wrong when you haven't actually heard them? I'm guilty of this too. And so is the rest of the world. It's called arguing. Try and practice this and when you actually start listening you may just like what others have to say.

Look, I'm not saying you're not allowed to get pissed off ever. Of course you are. When shit hits the fan, you flipping your lid doesn't label you a Bridezilla. Some chicks go out of their way to be easygoing and super laid back to avoid being called the awful B word and that's not good either. Because then nothing gets done! A happy medium is what you want. You want to be normal and not psychotic so when things go sour and you do lose your shit you're not slapped with the label. Be credible. Because someone who does lose it every seven seconds will not be taken seriously anymore. They become that person that gets mad about everything. They are just downright annoying. On the other hand, if you're a fairly normal person, who then gets angry when something goes wrong, people are a bit more sympathetic and inclined to help rectify the situation. Be that person. Always.

It's ok to settle. Yep you heard me right. Maybe not for the man you're going to marry or the dead end unfulfilling job where you reside eight hours a day for the next 30 or so years; but for your wedding wants. It's OK to settle for less than what you wanted or what you dreamed of because these 8 hours will be over before you know it and it's just not that big of a deal. If you've made all your dreams come true then hats off to you. If you just can't because of school, work, finances, kids, illness, whatever, it's perfectly fine. You'll get over it. Pretty bloody quickly in fact.

Reality check: I asked a cousin of mine if she wishes she did anything differently for her wedding a few years ago. Her response? "Who the fuck cares?" Why? Because she has two beautiful children who are her life. Her be all and end all. She doesn't give a shit about a wedding she had six years ago. Since then there have been first steps, first words, first hugs and kisses and memories that she'll cherish far more than her wedding day. That's the mentality you need to have when you go into planning. You won't necessarily think, "who cares", that will come after. But you will think, "big deal if I don't get the 8 tier cake" or "oh well I made a spelling mistake on the seating chart and now I need to dish out another $200 to get a new one printed and rush delivered"

"Too bad so sad that it's raining, someone get me some gumboots!" This should be your new mentality.

Let go of the things that are out of your control, stop being dramatic and roll with the punches. There are worse things in life than a wedding day that doesn't meet Kimye standards. Settle petals. If you don't let yourself get worked up and you let go of little miss perfect then you'll have a perfect day. It'll be just fine. One day does not define your marriage.

Scan this BARCODE to take the Control Freak Quiz!

10

Tacky Wedding Etiquette

SHIT NOT TO DO

Before you get all sensitive on me, let me just say there's nothing wrong with being frugal when it comes to your wedding. It's one day and there's no need to start selling off your belongings just to be able to afford it. I'm all for sensibility and finding cost effective ways to put on a lovely affair to celebrate your nuptials. Nowhere in that sentence, or in this book did I say to do that you need to be tacky. Not tacky in a satin teal linen kind of way but tacky in a distasteful way. Ok, both are unacceptable but we'll focus on the latter.

You know that bride who cuts corners everywhere? The Bridezilla in her rears its ugly head and she demands deals and discounts from everyone. She goes to friends and family barking demands expecting everyone to be a natural at flower arranging and graphic design just to save a dollar. It may be acceptable if she's on a budget and really needs all the help she can get. It's not acceptable when she's taking all that free time she now has and the extra cash over to Chanel to purchase herself an evening bag at $2500. When she puts everyone out just to make room in her budget for what really matters. Designer labels for her and herself only. Yes, yes, her day but doesn't mean she can be downright selfish and take advantage of people she calls friends.

Does that sound a bit like you? Perhaps you should make a bit of room in your spotlight and pay attention. Don't be a hypocrite. If you're going to be cheap, at least be consistent. Don't go crying poor to your friends when you very well know that your intentions are entirely selfish. If no one else has, I'll be the first to tell you that everyone thinks you're full of shit.

Take Maddy, for instance. Maddy was basically an egomaniac. I'm pretty sure she secretly thought her and her friends were the real cast of Sex and the City and she was Carrie. Leading up to her wedding she was trotting around on her high horse thinking her shit didn't stink and she was the most easy going laid back bride in history. Laid back with some seriously expensive taste. Nothing wrong with this of course, if you're willing to dig deep into your own pockets and fund this fantasy. Maddy wanted her besties in custom made designer dresses, she wanted a bachelorette party in a penthouse suite in the most exclusive hotel in the city with bartenders, strippers, you name it, followed by a night on the town. If that wasn't enough she also wanted a second bachelorette party in Vegas. No, she wasn't a descendant of royalty, nor was she a celebrity. She expected her girls to make her wishes come true on their dollar. Because it was HER wedding. How's that for super laid back? More like, vomit sundae.

You may love diamonds and labels and lavish trips because you live your life thinking you're a celebrity and that's great for you, but you can't expect your friends to jump on your bandwagon. Everyone is different. When you pop the question to your chicks you have to be aware of each and every one of their personal situations. One may be the Samantha to your Carrie and ready to participate in all you're lavish affairs, but the others may be a little less flexible. There's a reason you chose these girls and correct me if I'm wrong it wasn't the size of their bank accounts or their ability to party from dusk till dawn. As I stressed before, not everyone will stop their lives to gear up for your main event. Not everyone will put your wedding at the top of their list for 18 months. This doesn't mean you aren't important. It just means their lives are just as important. If your BFF can't fly to the other side of the world to celebrate your last week of freedom because she's got family obligations, don't turn your nose up at her. If you can't understand people's legitimate reasoning for not being able to partake in your festivities then you should take a hard look in the mirror and take a look at the shitty friend staring back at you. She's the only friend you'll end up having if you keep it up.

People have mortgages, babies, renovations and all kinds of other debts and obligations. You don't want to put anymore added pressure on the people that mean the most to you. Take dresses, for instance. If you've allocated $10,000 to pipe and drape the crap out of your head table so it can look like the King's Table, don't you think you can allocate a couple hundred on your bridesmaids dresses? I can sympathize with those of you that truly can't afford to pay everyone's way. You have absolutely no obligation to do so. However, with a massive budget and the best of the best of everything it's pretty low of you not to.

How about your wedding favours? Why are you holding weekly DIY workshops when you can just add an extra $5 per person to your budget (the equivalent of the back-up *Vera Wang* Veil you want but don't need) and have all your ribbons tied for you? Your girls will appreciate it, because right now, if you've got one making your invites, the other working on your candles and bridesmaid number 3 is working a second job just to keep up with all your requests, I can assure you, they are quietly losing their shit. Especially after they are expected to pay for their own dresses, shoes, hair make-up, nails, fund both your bachelorette parties which they are obligated to attend AND get you a wedding present on top. If you're lucky enough to make it to the end of the aisle with all your girls still by your side, I'll change my name.

Besides keeping your bridal party members happy and showing them you appreciate them by not being a complete dick head, it's important you treat your guests the same way. Do not, under any circumstances, make your guests pay for a single thing the moment they walk through the door. Specifically, the drinks. Cash bars are beyond tacky. These guests that you call loved ones got their hair done, nails done, bought a new dress, new shoes, got you a gift, could have gotten a babysitter or took the night off work just to be there for you. The most insulting thing you can do is have them paying for their own drinks. If they came over and you offered them a drink would you show them a bill and say "That'll be $5.50". I and all the wedding pros are in agreement that cash bars are a major NO NO.

Scan this BARCODE to read David Tutera's reaction to a cash bar

There is a way to cut bar costs but it's not asking your guests to reach for their wallets. One option is you could just offer beer and wine. There's nothing wrong with that and it's far less embarrassing. If you're set on offering liquor then another alternative is "closing" the bar during dinner. Just offer wine with dinner and once the speeches and formalities are over and the dancing begins the bar can open. Your guests won't really notice this as they'll be too busy eating your delicious food. I know that not everyone can afford a full premium liquor bar at their wedding. Those can run you anywhere from an extra $30-$100 per person. But there are many alterations such as limiting the selections.

This brings me to my next point. Letting your guests go home hungry. The exclusive reception that you HAD to host your wedding at means nothing if you can't afford to feed your guests properly. After they've dished out a week's paycheck to be there, although they're looking forward to seeing your glowing beauty, they're looking forward to a good meal. When they don't get one, that's what they'll be talking about. All the money you spent on your decor, your 8 tier cake, your photo booth and that 7 piece band will all be for nothing when all your guests remember is the rumbling coming from their empty bellies.

Solution: If you're set on that venue, you've got to make some cuts. Try a Friday night wedding or a Sunday brunch. Try a cocktail reception and state it clearly on the invite so everyone knows to plan ahead. This is all completely acceptable. Notice how I didn't say to try a Sunday night? That's because I'm not the biggest fan of Sunday night weddings. Sunday brunch, yes. Sunday night, when everyone is winding down and gearing up for their long week ahead, don't take that away from them. Not to mention, knowing a new work week is only ten hours away makes people quite somber. It certainly won't be the party you were hoping for as many guests will be dining and dashing. And holidays, stay away from them. There's nothing more irritating than looking forward to the few and far between long weekends you get, even fewer when you consider how many of them are in the summer, only to find that you have to go to a wedding. Sadly, long weekend weddings are associated with tight asses. Even if it's not the case, it pisses people off so much that they immediately judge. You took away

106

their weekend at the cottage, or their Christmas with their families so you could get married on the cheapest day of the year. Not a nice look.

Asking for monetary gifts. This is a major wedding faux pas. Some will beg to differ and throw every excuse under the sun as to why straight up asking for money is an acceptable request but this is very black and white to me. It's tacky. It's in bad taste. Don't do it. Don't do it for your bridal shower - the point is to be showered with gifts not cash. Don't do it for your engagement, and don't do it for your wedding. Same goes for the dudes - don't do it for your fundraiser. I mean, bachelor aka stag party. People shouldn't be obligated to pay you on your wedding day or for any event leading up to it. If they want to give you cash then great, happily accept and graciously say thanks but don't demand this. It's off putting. You're not providing a product or service, you're inviting them to a celebration. There shouldn't be a cover charge. If you can't afford to get married without it then don't get married yet or do it within your means. SIMPLE. Here's that poem I mentioned earlier that people think is acceptable to add to their wedding invitations:

Our home is quite complete now,
we've been together long.
So please consider our request,
and do not take us wrong.

A delicate request it is,
we hope you understand.
Please play along, as it will give
our married life a hand.
The tradition of the wishing well,
is one that's known by all.
Go to the well, toss in a coin,
and as the coin does fall,
make a wish upon that coin,
and careful as you do,
cause as the well's tradition goes,
your wishes could come true
So on this special day of ours,
the day that we'll be wed,
don't hunt for special gifts,
But give a gift of money instead.

As a wedding planner, I'm appalled by this. "Do not take us wrong"? They will. "Hope you understand"? They shouldn't. This is bad form and a big 'Fuck-No' in my books.

A new thing that has been circulating the last year or so is asking for outrageous gifts. Social media has really put unachievable things at our fingertips. We follow Kate Moss and Kim Kardashian only to hear that they put things like Hermes pillows and insanely expensive china on their registries. Imagine taking a glance at someone's registry and finding an $800 spoon on there? True story – Kim K did it:

Wedding number deux to Kris Humphries. Kate Moss was said to have a $6600 silk rug on hers! I don't know about you, but I think it's far more ridiculous for celebs to do it - if anyone can afford these things it's them. Wouldn't it be a little classier to donate to a charity?

Scan this barcode to see a few more of their outrageously expensive items:

According to Bride To Be Australia, a Brit who I won't name asked her guest for boobs on her registry. Yes, you read it right. BOOBS. She asked her guests to come together and fund her new double D's. She thanked her guests by saying, "My wonderful wedding guests have given me the greatest boost to my married life — new boobs!" How crazy is that?

I've just come around to registries in general. I use to be against them. I don't like the idea of asking guests for anything. I didn't have a registry for any of the events leading up to the wedding, or for the wedding itself. If I'm inviting people to an event I'm hosting I just don't expect gifts. We went out of our way to stress to our guests, especially our overseas ones, that we did not want gifts. But, leading up to my bridal shower my friends and family members were freaking out because they had no idea what to get me. Apparently, nowadays, people get annoyed if you don't register. We live in a world where people need guidance and they need to be told exactly what to do. I blame automated technology and social media. It's like we're all a bunch of zombies that don't have the ability to think anymore! So, for my baby shower I've bitten the bullet and I registered at Babies R Us. I did NOT however, register at Pottery Barn Kids where one teeny crib blanket costs $169. Keep this in mind when choosing your registry and what you put on it. Don't register for something stupidly expensive that you'd never buy yourself. Oh, and another tip, pick a store with many locations. I have a bridal shower coming up and the mummy to be registered at a remote boutique outside of the city. Pain in the ass.

Moving on to thank you notes. This was mentioned before but can't be stressed enough. Simply put, write your thank you cards ASAP. I never understand when I get a Thank You Card 6 months later. Back in the day it was because couples waited for the photographers photos but these days with same day edits, with your photos going up on their blogs almost immediately and all other instant forms of uploading your pictures, coupled with sites like Wedding Paper Divas or Minted who deliver your cards in 48 hours there is absolutely no excuse to wait so long. You squeeze all this money out of people and then literally the day after the wedding you don't have time to sit down and write out a few' thank you's'.

Plus, it's better to do this right away while you're still in wedding mode. As soon as a couple weeks pass, you're back from your honeymoon and back to reality, you've closed the book and there's no way you'll have any interest in re-opening it and doing anything wedding related.

Finally, back to the wedding day. Don't be a shitty host - take the time to see and thank all your guests. It's not their problem you invited 400 people. A good way of making sure you do get to everyone is by having a receiving line at the start of the night. During the cocktail hour while everyone is arriving is the perfect time to do this. If you have a small bridal party it doesn't hurt to have everyone up there greeting your guests. You can even assign tasks, for example, have a couple of bridal party members giving favours to your guests, have another couple in charge of guest book signing and another in charge of seating chart and showing guests to their seats. In the meantime you greet them as they come with your parents. This gives people a chance to personally congratulate you, compliment you on how beautiful you look, and most importantly gives you a chance to personally thank them for their generosity. You can never say thank you enough. Depending on the size of your guest list, this may take up to an hour and you may miss the delicious antipasto table but it frees up a lot of time during the rest of the night. Rather than rushing around through tables you can actually enjoy your meal! Then you can mingle at your leisure and if you happen to miss a few people it's not such a big deal because you've already spoken to them at the beginning of the evening. Having a receiving line doesn't mean you can ignore everyone all night and isolate yourself just because you've already spoken to them. Don't mistake this as a free pass to be a snob. It's still important to grab your hubby and do a few rounds to make sure everyone is enjoying themselves. Make sure you find a happy medium between mingling with your guests and partying it up.

11

The Long and Short of It

CHOSING BETWEEN A LONG OR SHORT
ENGAGEMENT

Congratulations on the anniversary of your long-term engagement.

someecards

Alright, ladies, it's crunch time. Out with the old long engagements and in with the new. Forget the traditional 18 month prep time because it's completely unnecessary. There are so many benefits to short engagements BUT, they're not for everyone. You need to be a few things; a master of organization and you must be flexible and open minded. Not a list person? Become one. If you can acquire these skills then there is no need to wait three calendar years to become a Mrs. I've always thought it to be absurd that it takes people so long to plan one day. Seriously, why wait?

Take one of my favourite couples Emilia and Jason. They came to me in December of last year and told me they were planning to wed in February. Yes, the following February. They had been living together for three years and now they had a little bun in the oven. She wanted to tie the knot before she was showing. They always had marriage in their future but were never in a rush; quite frankly they were already functioning as a married couple. Now that they were adding to their family they thought this would be the perfect time to celebrate. Times have changed now and couples situations are changing. 75% of couples live together before the question is popped. Another 40% go on to have kids before they marry. This makes the wait time for the ring longer and once they have that then there's no need to wait another two years to make it official. More importantly, the further along in your relationship you get, the less emphasis gets put on a big party. Peoples priorities are shifted as they get further into life and the responsibilities and challenges it throws at them. Getting married isn't a significant change in a relationship anymore.

Emilia and Jason's wedding date was eight weeks after they hired me and I was their second stop. All they had booked was the church and it was up to me to help with the rest. Challenge accepted. I explained to Emilia that although this was possible I wasn't about to start pulling miracles out of my Mary Poppins bag. I would create the most beautiful wedding but she needed to be open minded. Top 10 Toronto wedding venues were out of the question as they would be all booked up, custom made *Ines de Santo Couture* gowns weren't going to happen because we didn't have 20 weeks to order, and the decor would have to be minimal. She couldn't have been more on board. In retrospect, she was one of my most easygoing brides. She was a super busy real estate agent who did not specialize in weddings. She said to me, "Bess, you know best. I'm not a wedding planner; I'm a real estate agent. I'm not going to pretend I know about cakes and flowers so here's my budget, let me know what you need from me, and do what you gotta do." Music to my ears. I'm not saying I want brides to stay the hell out of my way so I can plan their wedding, but this mentality is such a breath of fresh air. She wanted the help. She was up to her ears with work and life, and now a baby on the way, and although she was super organized and probably very capable of planning this wedding in such a short time period, she wanted to leave it to the professionals. She was the ideal bride to be.

Everything I came at her with she was happy

with. I had shortlisted four venues for her 100 person guest list. We headed over to the first one, I always show my favourite first and it's almost always the last. This case was no different. We walked in and they were floored. It was a hidden gem in downtown Toronto. A private club that wasn't well advertized but absolutely perfect for their wedding day. Because this place was off the radar, not only were they available but the price tag was beyond reasonable for downtown. With a One King West feel, it was timeless and elegant. Absolutely perfect. They signed on the spot and we ventured down our list of things to do.

A benefit of having a short engagement is you don't have to pull teeth for help. Her friends and family we're beyond supportive and were offering a helping hand everywhere they could. So were my suppliers. I made some calls and got the bakeshop, stationary chicks and my florist in to see the venue a few days later so they can see the room in which they would display their creations. The ballroom had a beautiful elegant/vintage feel with pastel green walls with gold and light pink trim, stunning crystal chandeliers, this spectacular fireplace, and the ceiling had this remarkable gold detailing. It really was a site for sore eyes. We oohed and awed while we brainstormed ideas and our fairies went off to make magic.

On Emilia's end, her job was to make lists. I needed lists and contact information of her other vendors, names of her family members and bridal party members, guest lists with meal preferences and final numbers. She was unbelievable. She decided to ditch the traditional invites and go with email and phone calls. I do love invites as I've dabbled in this department myself, however when you only have a few weeks and you have to rely on snail mail to get them out and to get your RSVP's back, it's not so ideal. With two weeks to go she had a list of 96 yeses along with everyone's meal requests and dietary requirements. I was impressed. Never had I worked with someone this efficient and organized. And somehow, in between the madness she managed to find a dress. She went in with a completely open mind and walked out with the perfect dress. Off the rack. My favourite way of wedding dress shopping. It did help that she had the perfect sample size body. Not everyone, myself included, would be so lucky.

Here's the thing though, again – you can't be picky. If you have your heart set on something specific and you don't have time to get something custom made, you're going to have a pretty hard time finding it. You need to let it go. There is so much out there it's ridiculous. It's also good to keep in mind that the more choices you have the harder it is. The second Emilia found a dress she absolutely adored, she didn't say, "Let me put it on hold, I still have another 14 boutiques to hit, and then I'll come back to it if it's still the one." Who the hell has time for this? If you love it, it fits, you feel confident; you're twirling around like the seven year old you once were playing dress up then what's there to think about? There are that many beautiful dresses out there that it's just too hard to choose one, I get it. If you are like me and love all things pretty then my advice is, limit your options. I was beyond fortunate to have my sister and mom fly down to Melbourne to celebrate my engagement so I waited for them to go dress shopping. I started browsing online for wedding boutiques and after 5 minutes I was completely overwhelmed. I was in Australia, for one. I wasn't fully educated on who's who in the wedding world and the ones I knew of were way out of my budget. To top it off, everything in Australia is way more expensive than it is in North America. My sister wanted to take a trip to Sydney and start there. I entertained the idea until I called some of the boutiques and they didn't have openings for another three weeks. Jules and my mom would have been long gone by then so this wasn't an option. I found a couple of dress shops in Melbourne, jotted down the addresses and we were out the door. On our way to the first one, we walked by one that wasn't on my list and my mom said let's just start here. It was 37 degrees that day; I think she just really needed some AC. In we went and about 20 minutes in I was wearing my first dress. I had zero expectations because I was expecting to find it at one of the boutiques we were on our way to before this detour.

One glance in the mirror and I was sold. I think it was a combination of happiness and excitement. My family was there with me, I was getting married in just a few months to the love of my life and I was perfectly tanned after a really hot summer; this dress emphasized everything and I couldn't be happier with what was looking back at me. It didn't need any altering besides the length which I could take care of in Toronto when I got back and it could be ready in four weeks. I was leaving in seven. Perfect, I thought. That was it. We skipped the other shops and enjoyed the rest of the day on the beach.

Leading up to the big day you will see other dresses. Whether it be on Instagram or Facebook or other wedding blogs, it's hard to just shut off once you've picked your dress and never open another magazine again. You still follow Pronovias and Marchesa and they're uploading all kinds of insanely beautiful dresses. This might be hard to hear, but there will always be a better dress out there. That doesn't mean yours isn't perfect. There are so many different versions of beautiful. There are so many different styles. Empire, mermaid, a-line...the list goes on and on. You can't possibly have it all. It's ok to look at others and think they're beautiful, but you picked yours for a reason. You had that feeling in it and when you put it on again on the day of your wedding you're going to have that feeling again, except it'll be multiplied by a thousand. The latest trend or hottest designer doesn't matter. What matters is that you feel beautiful and confident. And that's another good thing about a short engagement. With a two year one, you got your dress in 2014 and by 2016, yours is ancient and you hate it because it's dated. A friend of mine got engaged two years ago. She's getting married early next year, therefore is having a two and a half year engagement. She bought her dress two years ago because naturally, you get engaged, you're excited and you want to go dress shopping ASAP! Well, she's watched three brides walk down the aisle in that exact same dress since then.

I absolutely loved my dress. I love how it looked and I loved how I felt in it. Have I looked at other dresses and said WOW I'd love to do it again in that! Absolutely. But do I regret my choice? Not for one second. Emilia had the same mentality. It so important to go with something you love. But it's also important to be realistic and know that you're not going down as the best dressed bride in history.

You can't get too attached to anything when it comes to your wedding. Unlike the backsplash for your dream kitchen that you'll be pretty close with for the next how many years, the details of your wedding are only with you for the better part of a day. So when you have a short engagement, you don't have a lot of time to get so attached to every single tiny little detail and that means no wedding withdrawals and no post wedding depression. When it drags on for way too long it becomes your life. You live and breathe baby's breath and when it's over you have no idea what to do with yourself. You could care less that you're married and all you want is something to plan! How about your long and happy life together?

You become far more grounded with a short engagement and you don't obsess over superficial things. And believe it or not, if you tend to be that type, short engagements change you. It changed me. For the better. I completely shocked myself. As a wedding planner I'm majorly detail oriented. I have to be or I wouldn't be good at what I do. Before I met Mark and I'd envisage my wedding I thought I'd have it all. Florals beyond florals, a head table fit for royalty with a venue overlooking the city skyline and a top of the line designer dress. Think Carrie Bradshaw almost wedding number one. Then when it came down to it, with everything else were we dealing with - moving, immigration, saying goodbye to family and friends and looking for jobs on the other side of the world - I just couldn't be bothered adding "intense wedding planning" to the list. I was exhausted just thinking about it. I was totally ok with something not so huge and elaborate. I just wanted it to be fun. And fun it was.

Not convinced yet? Here are some Long Engagement Myths:

No Stress
Some people think that the longer you have to plan

the better. That way you can pace yourself and really take your time figuring out the details. Wrong. The longer, the more stressful. First of all, the last 3 months are the only months you do anything anyway. Once you book the venue and a couple of the other big things you end up sitting on your ass and doing nothing for 14 months anyway.

More time to save.

Also a barrel of bullshit. While you're waiting around for those fourteen months for something to do, you're polluting your brain with all things wedding related. You're just adding more and more to the list of crap you don't need. You're saving more money so you're justifying spending more. The more time you have the more you spend, not the more you save.

Spend less by booking vendors early

Contrary to popular belief, the closer to the wedding you book, the more discounts you'll get. Emelia got her cake at half off, the venue lowered their minimum spend and the DJ also gave them a considerable discount because to them it was extra money they would have never made. Getting discounts is not a guarantee but it's much more likely than getting one when you're over a year out. If you try and negotiate with a vendor that far out, they'll just tell you to keep walking because the next bride will pay them what they want and she's right behind you.

You get ideas from others that get married while you're engaged.

Recipe for disaster. This is what makes you competitive. You lose sight of what you want and become obsessed with being better and more trendy than anyone else.

You get a longer exciting engagement period

Over rated. Marriage is so much better.

You get to know each other better

I never understood this rationalization. Isn't that called dating? If you still don't know how he sleeps or if he only brushes his teeth once a day then I think you should consider going back a couple steps before moving forward with a wedding. Look at Will and Kate. They were together forever getting to know each other. There was much speculation that something was wrong because it was taking ages but once he popped the question and their engagement was announced it was a quick 7 months before the royal wedding.

***

Aside from avoiding pimple breakouts and nervous breakdowns, there are plenty of other advantages of getting hitched in a hurry. This is not the year 1827 guys. Your husband to be is not expected to accumulate enough wealth and status to keep you. It's also not our parents generation where you can't have a sleepover with your boyfriend when you see him in your future. We're getting married much older these days, and as a result our loved ones who want to see us walk down the aisle are getting older. Most of our parents were all married in their very early twenties, some even in their late teens and a lot of them were fortunate enough to have their parents, grandparents and relatives there to witness. If you have the opportunity to get married sooner than later and granny can witness then do it. These are what our relatives live for as they get older.

Here's another fun fact: more grooms partake in the wedding planning when you're on a tight timeline. We all know that the boys aren't into weddings and besides what time to arrive and where to stand, their involvement doesn't go too far beyond that. Unless you're Mark. My husband wanted to be involved in all aspects of the planning. His thing was "a splash of red". He wanted a splash of red everywhere. It was weird. Moving on. Sometimes, to get your hubby-to-be involved you have to give them far less options. With fewer moths to plan, you have fewer options. You have very simplistic expectations and that way he's not rolling his eyes at the thought of helping you. He wants to help you because the finish line isn't ages away. You haven't overwhelmed him with all kinds of unimportant details and gone all Bridezilla on his ass for him to become uninterested.

Lastly, my number one reason why getting married on a short timeline is a good idea is because you just get to be married already! This might sound cheesy, but marriage is awesome. Even if you've lived together for ages, something changes after that day. All of a sudden you feel like more of a grown up. You're thinking about kids and bigger homes and minivans and you've entered a new chapter in life. Sure, back in the day it was like a whole new world getting married. You were sleeping away from home for the first time, you'd never seen anyone naked before and you were about to have sex to make another human being. But even now with all the modern twists in today's world, it's still different. You're no longer one person. You're a couple. The connection is on a whole other level. Communications change and consideration changes. You even find you're outside relationships change. It totally sucks losing a friend and I'm not saying cut the cord and move along you're married now. But, behaviours you once tolerated become a lot less tolerable and you tend to weed out the bullshit friends.

You and your partner end up respecting each other on a whole different level. You're not calling your bestie and ripping your husband a new asshole anymore. You protect your relationship more this way and you deal with your issues yourselves rather than airing out your dirty laundry to everyone else. You become this amazing duo.

So much changes, and life's too short so I say forget the endless months of prep to put on one day and concentrate on the years to follow.

"...I came here tonight because when you realize you want to spend the rest of your life with somebody, you want the rest of your life to start as soon as possible."

When Harry Met Sally

12

Entitlements: Wants vs. Needs

KNOW THE DIFFERENCE

My comedic idol Chelsea Handler said it best in one of her books and I could not have said it better myself when she wrote:

"It's not the concept of marriage I have a problem with. I'd like to get married too. A couple times. It's the actual wedding that pisses me off.
The problem is that everyone who gets married seems to think that they are the first person in the entire universe to do it, and that the year leading up to the event revolves entirely around them. You have to throw them showers, bachelorette weekends, buy a bridesmaid dress, and then buy a ticket to some godforsaken town wherever they decide to drag you. If you're

really unlucky, they'll ask you to recite a poem at their wedding. That's just what I want to do- monitor my drinking until I'm done with my public service announcement. And what do we get out of it, you ask? A dry piece of chicken and a roll in the hay with their hillbilly cousin. I could get that at home, thanks.

Then they have the audacity to go shopping and pick out their own gifts. I want to know who the first person was who said this was okay. After spending all that money on a bachelorette weekend, a shower, and often a flight across the country, they expect you to go to Williams Sonoma or Pottery Barn and do research? Then they send you a thank-you note applauding you for such a thoughtful gift. They're the one who picked it out! I always want to remind the person that absolutely no thought went into typing in a name and having a salad bowl come up."

— Chelsea Handler, My Horizontal Life: A Collection of One-Night Stands

Entitlement: I also like to call it delusion. Brides all over think that they are owed something and that they deserve this spectacular event starting from the proposal. You expect a proposal under the Eiffel Tower, an engagement as big as some weddings, a bridal shower that requires a second mortgage and then a bachelorette party on some exotic island with your besties, followed by a wedding fit for George and Alma Clooney. Then we can't forget the honeymoon in Mauritius in a private over-water bungalow at $2500/night for your honeymoon. Why? Because you deserve it. You're special. Just like mum and dad told you all those years. If you don't get what you want you turn right back into that bratty seven year old and have a temper tantrum. I've seen it with my own eyes and it's not pretty. Full blown tears, wails and snot coming out of an adult who is about to get married and is probably right around the corner from having children of her own one day. Do you know how ridiculous this is? You clearly have no idea how lucky you are. Now, this isn't your fault. It dates back to our grandparents.

Gen Y babies, pay attention. Our parents worked their asses off to have a better life than their parents had. Our grandparents lived in teeny tiny homes with 8 kids the size of some of your walk in closets. So when our parents worked hard and were rewarded with decent size homes they were left beyond satisfied. Their expectations were far lower than our inflated ones. Our inflated expectations are ridiculous because of social media now, however, they started with our parents convincing us that we are the most special thing ever to walk to planet. They got educations, they worked hard and it paid off. So that's what they taught us to do. Well kids, we live in a different world now. An education isn't as good as gold now because everyone has one. A great career now is nothing like what our parents had because back then cost of living was affordable. Now it's not nearly as relative.

So, here we all are, with this huge sense of entitlement thinking we are each special and better than the next person with our fancy degrees and huge egos. We worked hard (so we think - but really we have no idea), we are not satisfied with just a roof over our heads. We need the granite counter tops, the pool in the back with the three car garage and three cars that come with it. See where I'm going with this? Our parents were grateful. We're all spoilt brats. I'm in the same category so don't think I'm letting myself off the hook here. In reality, most of us don't know what working hard really means. My parents worked like three jobs each, I don't even know how that's possible. If we work an hour overtime we think we've earned a promotion.

Scan this BARCODE to read an article on why Gen Y babies are basically little shits all grown up in fancy suits now.

Then social media came along and royally screwed us all up even more. Now, rather than comparing ourselves to ourselves, we're looking at everyone else and saying, "Well everyone else has it, so I need it!" We can't distinguish the difference between wants and needs anymore because the bar is set so high, there's a blurred line between the two. And as I've said before, a lot of what people are advertising is all bullshit anyway because they've succumb to the pressure too. The only reason you're friend Jenny had the wedding of her dreams is because she took out a loan to fund it because her friend Rachel's wedding was on Style Me Pretty. If Rachel had it then she had to have it and if Jenny who's a plain Jane had it then how can you not? You're better than Jenny so it's time to put your foot down and start barking out demands of what you NEED for the perfect day.

I just threw up in my mouth a bit. Because we now live in a society where if we don't get married at the Royal York then we're hard done by. Did you hear the story that went viral on Facebook of the girl who publicly humiliated one of her guests for only giving her $100 as a wedding gift? How dare she, right? This poor bride went into debt, took a year and a half out of her life, basically sold her soul to plan the wedding of her dreams and feed her guests at $250 a plate and that woman had the audacity to show up with a measly $100? The nerve!

Seriously, if any of you can relate, put the book down and walk away. I've already lost you and there's no hope.

You're not entitled to a hefty gift, you're not

entitled to a horse and carriage, you're not entitled to anything! In the city of Toronto in order to get married you NEED a marriage license. This costs $117.10. The rest is all stuff. I'm not saying don't do it. If I really thought that then I'd be out of a job. I plan weddings. I love them. I'm just saying don't get all huffy and puffy if you can't get something you want.

Look at the weddings we're having now compared to the weddings our parent's had back in the 70's and 80's.

My mom rented her dress and the bridesmaids dresses, there was a simple church ceremony and no reception to follow. That was enough. There were no crazy expectations or Pinterest boards to follow. It was simple and just what she wanted. Her and my dad honeymooned in Niagara Falls. They didn't care for the latest hotspot where they could do some celebrity spotting and feel like one of them for five minutes. They didn't care. They were just grateful to get away after working around the clock day in and day out. They had much lower expectations so when at the end of the day they were satisfied.

This doesn't just apply to brides. It applies to our wonderful grooms as well. What part of the wedding festivities are they most involved in? Their bachelor party, of course. Ever heard of a little movie called "The Hangover"? Hands-down one of the funniest movies ever, yes. But it also put bachelor parties on a whole new level. Every guy now wants to go to

Vegas. Gone are the days when going out with the boys for one last hoorah was enough. Now it's Vegas and four days of clubs, pool parties, cabanas and bottle service. Some of these parties can run one guy about $5000 for one weekend. Are you kidding me? Every guy now thinks he's Bradley Cooper and that he's entitled to this. Hello?! Some of you have wives, fiancées, kids, or girlfriends that you're saving for a ring for. You're strapped for cash but somehow you can afford a VIP weekend.

Vegas, or any destination bachelor or bachelorette party is a complete luxury. It's not needed. It's super expensive, a huge commitment and not everyone can afford it. Nothing wrong with that. What's wrong is the pressure to be able to afford it. It's become the norm and nowadays if a guy doesn't get a trip halfway across the world then it's not a real bachelor party.

So what does he do? He holds one of those, in my opinion, completely unacceptable "stags" that his boys promote like a club. Tickets are sold to every Tom, Dick and Harry that he either knows or doesn't know. Can someone please explain how this is acceptable? Tickets are $80 each, it's open bar, there are prizes to be won, poker tables and hot chicks serving drinks. At the end of the night everyone leaves broke but happy because they've won iPads and big screen TV's but not as happy as the groom who just made $20,000 off their sorry asses. Um, that's not a bachelor party. That's called a fundraiser.

And it's pathetic. Then you see the groom's pictures on Facebook in Vegas with his friends washing down their Greygoose with Moet all with money that was raised from people he's never met before. How completely warped is all that? But everyone else does it, right? If they did it then he's entitled to it too. So it's acceptable. I just threw up in my mouth again.

How do you avoid being a bratty little Princess who thinks she NEEDS it all to be happy? Start with making a list. A wants vs. needs list. Think of your needs practically and really think about if you need the monogrammed charger plates for 450 of your guests before you put it on that side of the list. You'll be surprised to see how many of your "needs" turn into wants. Don't take this as me saying that because they're wants you shouldn't get them. Why shouldn't you? This is strictly to keep both your feet on the ground while planning your wedding. This is how things don't get blown out of proportion. You'll be surprised to see how many of your wants end up being omitted. This will help with keeping within your budget as well. Once you have enough to cover your costs on your needs then you can start having fun with all your wants.

You will still get carried away and emotions will run wild when you're trying on dresses or picking out wedding bands, that's a given. It's your wedding day and you should be allowed to spoil yourself here and there. This way just makes you a little smarter and totally conscious of your decisions. You know what you want and you know what you need. You don't feel entitled to anything, you just really want what you want and if it's within your means you're going to get it.

13

Keep Calm and Hire a Planner

Rather than spending your time stressing and worrying about every minor detail you should be celebrating your engagement. Venues, Florists, cake decorators, invites, photographers, celebrants, DJ's...where the hell do you start? You start with a wedding planner. I'm not just saying this because I am one. One reason I'm not too shabby at what I do is because I believe in what I do. You have no idea how much easier wedding planners make your life and how much money we actually save you! That's right, you heard me correctly. Save. We certainly don't work for free, but we incorporate our fee into your budget. You don't even feel it. So many people, especially grooms, have the misconception that wedding planners are a luxury for the rich and famous. False, my friends. At least half of my brides are on tight budgets.

Think about it this way: do you do your own taxes or do you hire an accountant? While many do their own, a lot of people opt for an accountant because they save you money. They know the ins and outs and little tricks of the trade to get you back some extra cash and even when their fee is taken into account you've still saved money in the end. Planners work the same way. I'm shockingly bad at accounting and may have had to repeat it a few times in college, but I'm certainly a pro at getting my brides deals and discounts while sharing my tips and tricks with them to save them money. Money that would be much better spent off the coast of the Bahamas on margaritas on their honeymoon. We make budget spreadsheets and show our couples where and how to allocate those funds, but most importantly, we keep them within those figures.

In addition to keeping your money just where you like it, we also save you some serious headaches. It takes an average of 250 hours to plan a wedding. A standard wedding. Throw in a little DIY and you're basically looking at a full time job. I'm sure you already have one so the last thing you want to do is deal with logistics you know nothing about. During the months leading up to a wedding I send and receive at least 20 emails a day per client. I deal with quotes, invoices, contracts, read all the fine print, make lists, check them twice and make sure everything's signed with all the T's are crossed and the I's dotted and I get everything finished on time.

As your wedding planner we are hired to organize the shit out of your wedding details. Yes, I'm sure you're organized too, but planning a wedding requires a whole new set of skills. We have lists and timelines and we've got this process down to a tee. Seriously, let us help you. For those of you who are indecisive, we can help in that department too. I have a pros and cons list stashed in my brain for every possible decision you'll need to make before you even know you need to make one. All wedding planners have a plethora of information that can magically help lift that weight off your shoulders.

When you hire a wedding planner you're also hiring a designer. You come to me with your favourite colours and it's my job to give you creative ideas within your budget that also paints a picture of who you are and what you want your big day to reflect to your guests. We have ideas that you would have never thought of. That's not to say you're not creative. Being a wedding planner is not just my job, it's my life. I've been planning, styling and executive weddings for over a decade and when I'm not doing that I'm researching. If I haven't been involved in a certain style of wedding, believe me I know everything there is to know about it. From religious, to same sex to Lord of the Rings themed (oh yes), to whimsical and everything in between, I've done it or I've seen it. Something could be rattling your brain for weeks and if you ask me the answer just rolls of the tongue. Your brain just doesn't go there, and why should it? It's not your job. I'm sure if I asked you anything about your profession you'd have a whole slew of knowledge to share with me while I stare at you dumbfounded. So rather than adding a whole new bit of information to your already full brain – let's face it, life's too busy these days – let someone else do the thinking for you.

As a wedding planner, I also act as your salesperson. I've already schmoozed your suppliers and as a result I've already gotten you the best deal possible. Fortunately for you, I've worked with them before and already have a great relationship with them. I know they'll deliver the goods and I know they'll do a kick ass job. The worst thing about hiring someone you don't know is that you have no idea how reliable or unreliable they are. You don't know their history, you don't know anyone that's used them and you don't know if they're taking you for a ride. I don't want to paint an ugly picture of the wedding world as most vendors are great to work with. But some aren't. With me you have a filter. I've weeded out the bad, I've collected the very best (in my opinion) and I've gotten competitive rates for you. My job is to connect you with the right people. I have a very extensive list of preferred vendors. It's quite long, and that's not because I go to anyone and everyone for discounts. It's because every couple is different and no two weddings are alike. Different budgets, different cultures, different visions, different styles and different personalities. I simply know who to connect with who; I'm like the *match.com* for weddings.

After finding myself in the middle of two people doing damage control and giving them couples counseling one too many times it occurred to me that we wedding planners also act as your shrink. Although many of you have an incredible support system made up of family, friends and even pets, their opinions may be biased. I can speak for most planners when I say, we give it to you straight. Your friend is going to side with you and tell you your beau is being completely unreasonable. His brother will side with him and tell him you're a total sociopath. I will tell you you're both nuts. My opinions aren't clouded with emotion and I'm completely unbiased. You definitely need someone neutral to help defuse situations.

Lastly, we are your day of crisis-averter and we take all the responsibility off of you. From the moment you wake up to when you unzip your dress at the end of the night, you are treated like the bride you should be treated as and you are not bothered because all communications go through us. This is a major advantage because if you knew half the shit we have to deal with on someone's wedding day you'd have an anxiety attack. I've seen wedding days that were ruined because shit hit the fan and it was all dumped on the couple because they didn't have someone to intercept and deal with it.

I have a spare foam cake in my car because I've seen cakes get delivered and then get splattered all over the floor. True story. I was at a venue doing the final once over and when I saw it happening it was literally like I was watching it in slow motion but I was frozen. I couldn't stop it. The caketress placed her creation on the table and left. I was on the other side of the room placing the favours on each setting and then I heard it. A snap and I just see the cake sliding down the table plummeting to its death. I was too far away, I tried to scream but it was too late. I stood there and just stared at it thinking of that episode of Friends with Rachel and Chandler on all fours trying to salvage the cheesecake from the floor and then I went into overdrive. I called the bakeshop and they hurried back with a fake cake and some extra icing. I plucked some flowers from the centerpieces and got to work. After the mess was cleaned up and the topper was placed on top, it didn't look the same, I'm not David Copperfield, but it looked pretty damn good. I brought the cake back to the stand - I walked to the cake stand with the cake raised like I was Rafiki presenting the new born Simba. It was pretty marvelous.

At another wedding, the ceremony was about to start and the celebrant was still not onsite. I was livid. The bride was naturally a bit of a high-strung person to begin with, so I could not tell her what was going on. I told her to hang out upstairs in her hotel room and I'd get her when we were ready. I said that It's OK to make the groom sweat a little and people usually expect things to start a bit late. The celebrant kept calling me with bullshit excuses about the traffic. She was stuck about a block away and I couldn't help but give her an earful about how unacceptable this was! This is Downtown Toronto and there's traffic. PLAN AHEAD! She kept going on and on about this blockage and that lane closure. I told her to shut the hell up and tell me exactly where she was. This woman was out to lunch. She didn't know north from south and it was impossible to try and explain to her how to get to the venue from where she was.

Finally I said, "Stay where you are, I'm coming!" I threw on my flats, gained my composure, and told the groom to hang tight and greet a bit more, we'd be starting in 5 minutes. I ran outside and down the street to the celebrants car, yelled, "Get out!" and jumped into the driver's seat. Barely allowing her to close the passenger side door and buckle up, I sped through some side streets and maneuvered my way back to the venue in two and a half minutes flat. I knew the back routes because, unlike her, I was prepared. I did many site visits leading up to this day and I made sure I knew of alternate routes in case there was traffic or road closures.

I practically launched her through the back entrance, took a deep breath, and headed upstairs to get the bride. She was all smiles. She had no idea what just happened or what could have happened. The celebrant got her shit together and the ceremony started and ended without a glitch. Despite her incompetence with driving and taking direction, it was a beautiful ceremony.

Alongside my foam cakes , my emergency kit, and my Olympic sprinting skills, I have all kinds of things with me at all times. One of my poor dear couples had the absolute worst weather. It was like a freak storm in the middle of June. They got drenched during their first look photos and my bride was devastated. They were meant to walk down the aisle in one hour and she looked worse than someone who was really hungover from partying and then crying all night after a breakup. We had serious work to do. While her bridesmaids were freaking out and running for cover, I grabbed the very soon to be Mr. and Mrs. and threw them in the limo bus. As your planner I have no emotional attachment to your wedding. Don't take that the wrong way, I'm not heartless, we've probably bonded and grown quite fond of each other. What I mean, is I'm not joining in on the pity party and crying my eyes out because my hair's soaked. I'm already in survival mode.

Out came the perfect clear oversized umbrella that also looks amazing in photos from my neverfull car, some chalk, my tide to go stick, a portable blow dryer and my assistant who I got to strip down to nothing. This may sound strange to you but my assistant is a male (I always like to have someone available for the boys) and he happened to be a similar build to the groom. He gave him a clean dry suit while I got to work on the bride. I cleaned her dress with a combination of Tide, Soda Water and bottled water, I blow dried her and disguised the hard to get out stains with the chalk. She looked like a blowfish from her panic attack so I dabbed some hemorrhoid cream under her eyes to eliminate the bags (yes totally works), touched up her makeup and hair and voila. Like it never happened. If I wasn't there, there was no way any of her girls would have kept it together to come through for her. Not in a selfish way, just in a "Oh my God, my hair! My Dress! I've never dealt with this crap before!" kind of way.

Things will always go wrong at a wedding. I've never been to one where nothing was forgotten. Whether it be a major catastrophe or something minor, it'll happen. Even at my wedding there were things that I forgot. Even though this is my profession, I hired a planner as well. There was no way I'd be my own wedding planner on my day no matter how good at it I was. You only get one wedding - hopefully. And you don't want your brain in 6th gear all day with mental images of lists or timelines other things you hope you didn't forget to do. My wedding planner was my savior. He was my brain for the day. I didn't even have to say anything, one minute I'm thinking, "Shit, did I leave my veil somewhere?" There he was behind me holding it. We went to a bar between the church and the reception and he was there keeping time so I didn't have to. I don't think I knew what time it was at any point in the day. I didn't know and I didn't care to. Because if speeches were happening at 7:16 pm after the first course was served it wasn't my problem to keep time. He made sure everyone was where they were supposed to be when they were supposed to be. Our reception started at 6:00pm and we were finished taking photos and back there with 15 minutes to spare. I didn't feel rushed for one second of my wedding day. I didn't have to watch the clock or set an alarm to know when we were to say our speech because I was graciously told when I had to do anything. I got so use to this treatment that I literally forgot to go to the bathroom all night. No one told me. Long story short, when I took by dress of at the end of the night I looked like I was 6 months pregnant.

One couple who didn't hire me told me it was because they wanted to handle everything on their own. They thought it would be fun to embark on this journey solo. They wanted to do all the research and make their own decisions. They thought it would be a breeze. Ha! I'm no doctor and my job doesn't exactly require me to perform complex surgeries but I can tell you first hand that wedding planning is not always fun. They pictured strolling through cake shops and feeding each other cupcake samples and frolicking through greeneries and meadows whilst picking the perfect flowers. What they forgot to imagine in their little fairytale were boring contracts and fine print, doing seating charts and keeping track of their never ending to do list while juggling their jobs and their daughter. There's nothing romantic about going through a year of extra tasks and just wanting the wedding to be over before it even begins.

Julie, a newlywed who wished she had hired me recently connected with me again after referring her sister to me. She gave me an earful as to why she wished I had pinned her down and force her to take on my services. She said that she had never argued more with her husband than she had leading up to the wedding. It was just too overwhelming. She was getting into trouble at work because she was doing wedding research on the job and after all that she still wasn't satisfied with the vendors they hired. She was running around the day before the wedding trying to find a string quartet because the one she hired hadn't returned her calls in over a week. They had literally just disappeared on her. She had just randomly found them on Craigslist and before that had never heard of them nor heard any reviews on them. This is where a wedding planner would have been a lifesaver! Luckily though, she told me the day was great and nothing went wrong but she spent a lot of it making sure everything was perfect and worrying that something would go wrong. You just don't want to deal with any of that crap.

As wedding planners, we've seen it all, we know how to prepare and we have contingency plans on standby. Take my advice and put the stress of planning and executing your wedding day in the 'too hard basket' by hiring a pro. You will thank me when your day comes and you have all the time in the world to dance, eat, mingle and enjoy every second of your special day.

To sum it up, we are your personal assistant, your creative designer, your stylist, your organizer, your time keeper, your coach, your go to person, we're your tablet, your financial advisor, your shrink, your buffer, your bomb diffuser, your money saver and time saver, your Google, your hustler, your food critic, your conscious and your subconscious, we're your friend, your family, your confidant and we're also your crisis averter. We're your legal aid, your real life Mary Poppins and we charge a fee that you are completely unaffected by because we incorporate it into your budget.

14

There's No Such Thing as The Perfect Anything

ACCEPTING IMPERFECTION AS PERFECTION

"There is no such thing as a perfect wedding. A wedding is about the love that surrounds the couple and it tells the story of the bride and the groom. If the wedding allows the guests to be transported to an emotional place they never thought they could be before, that's a perfect wedding. If they can walk away seeing something they've never seen before, that's a perfect wedding. If you learn more about the bride and the groom and their story, that's a perfect wedding. It's not about how beautiful the flowers are, how great the food is, how big the cake is, how beautiful the dress is; those are things you have to do. It's about walking away with an emotion you didn't think you had."
- David Tutera on A Perfect Wedding

There isn't. And frankly, who gives a shit? It's time to learn how to be perfectly imperfect and once you accept what I'm about to tell you, you'll be on your way to a stress-free engagement followed by a stress-free day. Shit's going to go wrong. There's no doubt about that. Despite your efforts to control everything, micromanage the crap out of your loved ones and pay microscopic attention to every tiny little details so the wedding days is PERFECT - it won't be. Ask any bride out there and I'll change my name if one of them says their wedding day was perfect and went on without a glitch. It may not be major, but something will go wrong, something will be forgotten or something will be missed. Accept it from now and you won't be beside yourself when it happens.

There's a lot of bullshit out there. Endless pages of blogs or articles that say things like "If you see each other before you walk down the aisle it's bad luck". Look, it's a cute tradition not to see each other, however, seeing each other beforehand also has it's perks. It's convenient, for one. You can take your photos first so you're not rushing around like a lunatic in the 6 minute window you have between the ceremony and the reception. Some couples even have breakfast the morning of and spend the night together the night before. Nowadays with so many couples opting to live together first it's really not a big deal to see each other before the big day.

On the other hand, I personally like the tradition because there's so much emotion in that one moment when the bride's in sight and the groom gets the first look. This wave of emotion hits them both at that moment and you can literally feel the love between these two people. It's fucking delightful. And the lead up is exciting.

My husband and I lived together before we got married and it was nice to take a step back in time and sleep separately. You almost feel like you're flying the coop again and it's kind of nice. That aside, it's not "bad luck" to see each other if you choose to do so before the big walk down the aisle. Back in the day it was said that the couple was FORBIDDEN to see each other before the wedding so the groom didn't have time to change his mind when he saw his bride. True story, but times have changed.

Arranged marriages are few and far between these days and although this was something to worry about then, I don't think that's the case anymore. So if you happen to be getting ready and your hubby to be walks in on you and sees you in your dress just don't sweat it. Your day is not ruined, your life together isn't doomed to unhappiness and I highly highly doubt he's going to freak out and go running. Your day will still be perfect if you just embrace what comes at you and just roll with the punches.

I'm a Virgo, in other words, a perfectionist. I can be a complete nightmare when I'm working on something. I get fixated and sometimes I won't look up from what I'm doing until it's perfect - or until it's

5:00 am. It drives my husband crazy. Regardless of this very annoying trait, when the unexpected hits there's nothing I could have done and nothing I can do to avert the crisis. The laptop I used to write this book is a piece of garbage and if the cord gets pulled out even for a second the whole thing shits itself and shuts down. Yes, that totally happened and of course I hadn't saved my work in a while because I was "in the zone" and just like that in the span of half a second I lost three hours of work. How did I avoid having a complete melt down? Well for one, I have a sense of humor. Having a temper tantrum was not going to get my work back so I had to laugh at what a complete idiot I was and just start over. I looked at the plus side. There's always a plus side. Mine was that this part of the book wouldn't exist and the pages I rewrote were actually better than the ones that were erased. And the last plus was that I finally got with the times and now I write in a program that automatically saves your work.

When disaster strikes like your wedding cake melting a little or your curls falling because it's humid just lighten up, laugh it off and move along. It's not that bad. And if you're going to get that worked up over such a tiny little thing while there are people in the world experiencing real problems and real tragedies then I suggest you check yourself. And just wait until kids come along, if you chose to have them. If you can't handle a little hiccup then what are you going to do when life slaps you in the face with a whole other basket of stress down track?

Take rain on your wedding day. I've planned a lot of weddings where out of everyone's control except mother nature's, it rained. I've dealt with brides who were amazing sports, threw on a pair of gum boots and embraced their inner kid and I've dealt with brides who let some water set the bitter mood of the day right from the moment they woke up to the moment they took of their shoes. It's sad.

One girl I know still talks about how it rained and ruined her wedding. Every single time we're at a wedding she'll bring up how the couple is either so lucky because the weather held up or how she can totally relate to how the bride felt if it was raining. It's draining. She still thinks she's the most hard done by individual because four years ago it rained on her wedding day. She's been on a trip around the world since then and has popped out a beautiful baby; she's married to the most fun loving guy and she's probably one of the luckiest people that I know for a million other reasons but she still holds on to that rain as the worst thing that could have ever happened and as a result she's just generally unlucky. That just goes to show how lucky she actually is if that's the worst thing that's ever happened to her.

If it rains, just turn the negative into a positive. It doesn't change who you're marrying and why you're marrying him. And not to mention - the photos. The BEST wedding photos I've ever seen have been on rainy days. Fun fact: photographers love overcast. It's the best lighting for them. Another plus - you're not squinting in all of your photos or sweating from the blistering hot sun. Or worse, wearing sunglasses in your photos. Men in Black has come and gone. It's NOT cool anymore. You don't look 'badass'. Anyway, here are worse things in life than a bit of rain or shitty weather, be grateful.

Accept the fact there is no "perfect". Learn to take things with a grain of salt, laugh it off and most importantly, let it go. Leave the "if it were me I would have…" at the door because your vendors, your friends and family, they're all human. As crazy and as much of a perfectionist as I am, I make mistakes too. Keep it classy and keep your shit together. Nothing's worth mascara all over your face and puffy eyes - the wedding day is one day yes - but the photos will last forever. Master these traits and you will have perfect. You'll have your perfect. And that's the best kind.

15

Aloha...The Destination Wedding

SHOULD YOU OR SHOULD YOU NOT WED
ON FOREIGN SOIL

This is something I wish I did and I think I speak
for every couple when I say that. Once all the hype is
over, all the money's spent and we're married but
broke we all turn around and say, "If I could do it
again, I'd go to Hawaii, take 20 people, get married
for a third of the price and get a vacation out of it."
No, I'm not saying I'd change anything about my day.
I don't regret anything, I absolutely loved it, but
whether I got married on a beach, in my basement, or
the Palace of Versailles, at the end of the day I'd be
married. That's what it's all about. Not just throwing a

party.

I love the idea of a destination wedding. I love it so much we actually considered it. Then we went through a whole list of pros and cons and realized it wasn't for us. It's awesome, but not always ideal. On the other hand, it can be super ideal and if you're ticking all the boxes in the Pro's column then I say go for it.

Here's the list we went through and that I go through with all my clients if they want to entertain the idea of saying "I Do" on foreign soil.

First question: Are you looking at hosting your wedding on neutral ground? This is something that inter-country, interstate or inter-city couples consider.

Mark and I, for example, are from two different ends of the Earth. Rather than shipping everyone from one end of the world to the other we thought, "Maybe we should do something like Thailand or the Mayan Riviera or more conveniently Hawaii (halfway)?" There were a lot of pros to consider like it would be fair that way and there would be more of a balance of attendance. When you do it in one or the others hometown then you have about 20 from one side and potentially 100+ guests from the other side. Another pro is everyone gets a real vacation in a new place. Con: you only have that small window of time with them. This was a big factor in putting this point in the con basket. We chose to get married in Toronto because family members like his sister and parents came for nearly a month. That's much longer than the week you get on an island.

Moving along, destination weddings mean smaller guest lists. Again, this can be a good or a bad thing depending on what's important to you and what you are or are not willing to sacrifice. Depending on the time of year and your guests commitments you could potentially only have a handful of people at your wedding. To some this is a huge pro. Weddings don't have to be this insane thing that people make them. Lavish 400 person events with six figure budgets. Some people want a very small intimate, no fuss affair with the few people they hold dear to them. If you're lucky enough to have those important people there then who cares about the rest? No offense. Not to mention this is a huge money saver. Weddings nowadays average at about $32,000 in Canada according to Wedding Bells Magazine. Destination weddings will run you well under $10,000. Smaller guest lists mean much lower costs and with numbers in the double digits you'd be more inclined to spend more per person. That's when you can have fun with decor and food selections. If I were having 30 people at my wedding I'd be happy to spend $7000 on the whole event. That number may be staggering to you because you think about it as around $230 per person to get married on a sandy beach but you can't look at it that way. You have to look at it is you just saved about that much per person on the other hundred or so guests who aren't in attendance. The ones you probably see once a year.

Small weddings are more intimate but they can be just as fun. The reality is out of the 200 people you have at your local wedding, only about 10-20% of them are the ones who will be partying it up on the dance floor and half of those are the ones you see on a regular basis. The rest, no offense again, are just fillers.

This conveniently brings me to my next point. Reduced costs. Although I don't regret my wedding, the tiny thought that we'd be $50,000 richer definitely crosses my mind. Crazy amounts of flowers and decor, designer dresses and shoes, paired with designer bridesmaids dresses and luxury custom cakes are all insanely beautiful, but at the end of the day, it's just stuff. None of it symbolizes the love you share with your soon to be hubby. Somehow during your engagement you can justify spending alarming amounts of money. Then you turn around a few days later and say, "What the hell was I thinking??" Take the chargers. The plates that go under the plates that you eat off of. I had a bride that spent $8 per charger for 260 people. Do the math. It's an all inclusive vacation for two to the Bahamas. Or it's a third of a destination wedding budget. When you're getting married on a sandy beach with a naturally beautiful backdrop, things like that don't matter. You don't do chargers because you just don't care. You don't do decor because a picturesque island is enough. You don't do designer shoes because you are walking down the aisle barefoot or with some funky foot jewelry. All these costs add up and in a tropical setting they're just nonexistent.

Vacation! Um, the main reason to wed away. Forget wedding day, hello wedding week. It's like a weeklong celebration on the island of your choice with the people you love. Rather than running around before the big day you can lounge by the pool or beach with a cocktail. And most importantly, you have more time to spend with your guests. On the wedding night you have eight hours to run around and thank everyone. On island time you can do it at your own pace over the week while you spend quality time with them. Just make sure you either stay on a few more days for the honeymoon or choose a different location altogether. The last thing you want is remembering your honeymoon with your whole bridal party and family!

One con that's usually the breaking point for most couples is that oldies and other loved ones can't make it. With the average age to wed at 29 years old for females and 30 for males, we're lucky if our parents are well enough to fly let alone our grandparents. This is a huge deciding factor. This is what it came down to for us. Marks grandparents were already missing out because they couldn't make it 10,000 miles to Canada so we didn't want to deprive my grandmother as well who would have not been able to fly down south. And it's not only the seniors that may be missing out. When you do get married miles away there's a possibility the closest people to you won't be able to make it.

My friend Andrea was asked to be in a mutual friends bridal party for her wedding in Mexico. This girl was super pushy and just assumed that she'd be able to make it. Right off the bat it was, "Oh my God, you HAVE to be there!" Well, that's not really fair. If you're not willing to pay your friends and family's way then you can't oblige them to be there. Andrea was super stressed about it for ages until she finally got the nerve to tell her friend that she couldn't get the time off work nor could she really afford it. Well her friend flipped her lid. Basically labeled her the most selfish person ever. Pretty sure she was the selfish one. Financials aside, there are so many other things that need to align to allow your near and dear ones to get away for an impromptu vacation. Sometimes it just can't be done. You have to be OK with it.

Another con is that there are so many legalities and paperwork you have to deal with when you get married in another country. If you chose a resort, the wedding package usually comes with a wedding planner that takes care of these things. If you're getting married in a church for example, then it becomes a bit trickier. You don't want to come back to your homeland to find that the wedding wasn't legit and you're not actually married. My advice is either chose a resort that takes care of everything for you, hire a wedding planner back home that specializes in destination weddings or another option is having a small ceremony at home first. Then the one on the beach - or wherever else you decide to wed - is more of a show since you're already technically married. I like this idea because if you have the ceremony at home first you can still involve the ones that have to miss the vacation to follow. That way everyone's happy. This also works when you want to get married in a church or religious institution. Sometimes, going to somewhere like Cuba and finding a church or synagogue that practices your religion is tricky. You don't know the priest, you don't know the legalities and requirements of getting married in that country and it could end up being a huge pain in the ass. I know a lot of people who have come back from their destination weddings only to find that they're not actually married!

So, tying the knot on home soil in the religious institution of your choice, not only allows you to have those that can't make the trip to your destination wedding to be there, it saves you a headache. This way, you get the best of both worlds.

Another enticing pro is that destination weddings mean stress free and simple. Some can be really simple. My cousin got married on the beach at an all inclusive resort in the Dominican Republic and then had a simple lunch in the resort's restaurant where other vacationers were enjoying their lunches as well. Whether you do that or rent out a private venue it's almost always a buffet style, it's not formal and the food is never really first class. Does any of it really matter though? Sometimes little details can be tacky but again, who cares? If you're not one to roll with the punches and you're not one to leave the planning to someone else miles away then I'd put this point in the con bucket. The reason these weddings are simple and stress free is because you're literally allowing the resort staff or on site wedding planner take control of your day. They're using local vendors, local food, that you've never seen or tasted and you're not going to know what to expect until it's too late. You're choosing things from your side of the world based on photos only. It will not be what you pictured when you get there. It will still, of course, be beautiful. And while someone else is planning your wedding from another country, you're doing what really matters. Spending quality non wedding related time with your fiancé and the people that you love.

Finally, the biggest con in going out of your postcode is that it's super costly for your guests. Sure, it's cheap for you, you're spending a third to get hitched on the beach but they've got to fork it out. This factor majorly downsizes your guest list and inconveniences those that are almost obligated to be there.

Your destination wedding is the perfect excuse to visit a place I'm not really dying to see.

someecards

When I had my engagement party in Australia for example, my sister and mother kind of had to be there. My sister was basically interning at the time and she had low funds. I certainly couldn't pay for her trip but I expected her there. It's not really fair. Whether it's a short or long flight away it's a pretty big financial commitment to ask of people. If you're entertaining the idea you have to ask those you 100% want there if they can make the trip. When we dragged thirty Aussies to Canada for our wedding we made sure that those important to us could make it. It's a big ask. And not to mention the burden of guilt you carry when they commit.

The boys in the bridal party, with the exception of my best friend, were all Aussie and they all had significant others. For flights alone they each had to pay over $4000 per couple. Then you add accommodation and spending money on top and it's a pretty pricey trip. We felt hugely terrible that we were putting all these people out so much. I'm forever grateful and humbled by their efforts but there's no way I can ever repay them. It's a lot to carry. We were very, very lucky that they were all in a position to come. We considered it the other way and it just wasn't feasible for most of my side to make the trip. Basically, Aussies save their money and love to travel. They are prepared to save all their pennies and pay more for vacations because Australia is way further to the rest of the world.

North Americans on the other hand, like quick cheap trips. The thought of a flight to the other side of the world is ludicrous. Not to mention overly expensive. When we pay under $1000 for an all inclusive trip to Mexico it's hard to justify spending over $2000 for a flight alone! We had to consider all these things when choosing a location.

Each situation is different and it's important to sit down with your fiancé and go over all the pros and cons of wedding away. If your bridal party, family and friends can't afford it and you can't fork it out then you may have to consider alternatives like exchanging your vows on home soil. Yes, you have your heart set on a destination wedding but what's a wedding celebration without at least most of those you love to witness it?

Have you ever considered eloping? This is something every single person says at some point when planning their wedding but there are few who actually do it.

Let's elope and piss everyone off equally.

Here's a pros and cons list to help you decide!

Pros	Cons
You'll save a ton of money	People will be hurt or offended and may label you as selfish
No hassle planning	You may potentially ruin your relationships with your inlaws
It's old fashioned and romanitc	You may be a disappointment or not what you expected
It's fun and spontaneous	You may have regrets after that you didn't have a wedding
It can be super casual if you're a "no fuss" kind of couple	Your families miss out on a very special day
There won't be any family drama to worry about	You don't get any gifts
More intimate and focused on just the two of you	You don't get an album or professional wedding photos
Focuses more about being in love and committing rather than throwing a party	No party or memories with anyone - it's just you two.
No nosy family opinions	Can't have any traditions like your dad walking you down the aisle
You get to tie the knot right away	You don't get to enjoy an engagement period
No religion or culture battles	You may offend religious of family values

In the blank template jot down your own list!

Pros	Cons

16

Stress You Can't Avoid

SEATING CHARTS AND FAMILY DRAMA

Unless you've done it, you have no idea how hard it is to arrange the seating plan for your wedding. IT'S THE MOST STRESSFUL PART! Not to mention, you can't get this over with and tick it off your list from the beginning. That would be too easy. This can only be done once you get your RSVP's back so first things first. Get your invites out three to four months in advance. Yes, four months is a bit of a stretch but it's better than being late. Make sure the RSVP date is at least five weeks before the wedding day. This gives you one week to chase up late replies (which there will be) and then a solid month to deal with this nightmare.

Another thing that sucks about this task is that you can't pawn it off to anyone else. Even if you've hired a Full Coordination Wedding Planner, you've got to do this yourself. We don't know your friends. We don't know your family. And we don't know the drama. Therefore, I don't have a magic plan that will make this totally painless but I do have some tips that will keep you from wanting to scratch your eyeballs out.

First, consider unconventional seating arrangements. That means accept the fact that the room won't be symmetrical. Yes, I like symmetry and perfect clean cut looking layouts too - I'm a wedding planner! But the faster you get over this the faster you'll be thanking me. Here are your table options:

60" Round 6-8 people   72" Round 10-12 people

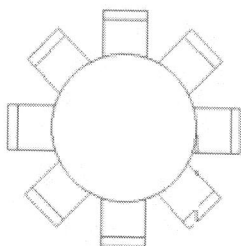

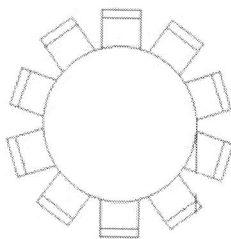

8 ft Rectangle tables

Square Tables 8-12 people

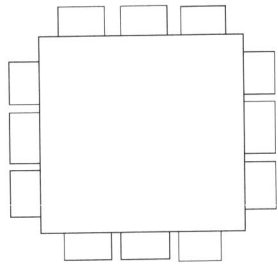

These can be lengthened according to preference

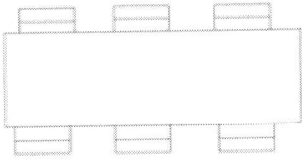

You certainly have more options but these are the basics that I like to work with. With these four options alone you have many options and a whole lot of flexibility with how many people you can put to a table. Not every table will have those perfect four couples that go perfectly together unfortunately. I had incorporated two long tables at my wedding and always recommend this to my brides. I had one long table of 26 friends and another long table of 23 cousins (I told you I had a big fat Greek family). With long tables you can deal with the joys of odd numbers. If you have a couple of randoms at the end that aren't assigned seating yet and you're stuck you can just extend the long tables. This ends up being a life saver. It's so much better that playing musical chairs and rearranging the entire plan for two people!

Now, you have your selection of different tables,

how the hell do you put it all together?

Before you even begin to play teacher and allocate people to designated seating, make sure you ASK your friends and family (at the very least the ones close to you) who they would like and would not like to be seated with. You may not like the idea of giving people the option because it over complicates things, but it's better than doing it yourself and having a conflict on the day. I sat down with each of my parents and asked for their guidance. My parents are separated so I had to take some family issues into consideration. This part is annoying and can't be avoided. If you're lucky and don't have to deal with this then count your blessings. If you do then just get it over with. But always remember you can accommodate to a certain point.

There will come a time when you have to put your foot down and say "Mom, I'm sorry but putting your ex-mother-in-law at a table outside of the room is not an option." Always remember that even though people may have unresolved issues and may not like certain situations, it's your wedding and they're adults. Mom and dad can put the claws away for one night and act decent for you. You can't and most certainly will not be able to please everyone. You can also work these details out way ahead of time. You may not know if Auntie Mary twice removed is coming to your wedding but you'll know if your parents, siblings, close relatives and friends will be attending. As soon as you know make sure you get their requests so you can accommodate as best you can.

Now that that's sorted, you have to literally seat everyone. I'm just learning how to incorporate my iPad and how to use all these crazy apps so if you're a techie then I'd recommend 3D event designer. Your wedding planner will have this also or something similar. It's like the Bible of seating plans. If you have a wedding planner then let them deal with it. What I tell my non-techie brides to do is to do it manually and I then input everything into my programs.

To do it manually and in my opinion, the easiest way possible, is start by writing every guests name on a post-it note. Then get out your kindergarten skills and your scissors and cut shapes of the tables you'll be using. Number them and start arranging people. The stickers make it easy to move people around. I know this sound ridiculously easy but it's amazing how people tend to over complicate things.

Things to keep in mind are babies and kids. They're better off being at the back or at the end of a long table if they need a booster seat. Kids between the ages of 6-12 years old can be at their own table in my opinion. Throw them a colouring book or a couple of tablets they can play games on and you'll be surprised how well behaved they'll be for the duration of dinner. And, their parents will be thanking you.

One last fun point is accommodating dietary requirements. Gone are the days when it was chicken or beef. You just ordered half of each main course and alternated the servings. If they didn't like what they got they switched. Now, there's vegans, veggies, lactose intolerant, dairy free, nut free, gluten free, garlic free, allergies to shellfish, starch, butter and everything else under the sun. Luckily, the venue usually handles these but it's very important you give them the correct info. Make sure you add a "Dietary Requests or Allergies" line on your RSVP for your guests. You'll also enjoy some of the responses you get back. Some people take this opportunity to customize their meal by requesting a specific meat, side dish (hold the onions and go easy on the garlic) and dessert. Be sure to take a photo of those and put it on Facebook so everyone can see how ridiculous they are. It's not a restaurant, it's a wedding. Once you've sorted through the request and have thrown out the irrelevant ones, give the venue a clear indication of where those guests are seated. Some venues want you to indicate it clearly on the place card for the servers to see and others are happy with just the name and a list of guests with their associated table number.

Finally, for the head table, have fun with this. There's no right or wrong. If you just want a sweetheart table then go for it. If you have family dramarama then this might be a good way not to have any parents at the head table so it's fair. If you want to have the bridal party and their spouses then great. Just bridal party? Fine. Whatever you do, just make sure your back isn't to your guests.

In conclusion, give yourself as much time as

possible and don't sweat the seating plan. It will certainly have its downs but you've gotten this far and it's the final month. Enjoy your last month as a Miss and take everything that comes with this hurdle with a grain of salt. Your guests are adults, they'll deal with your placement for a few hours.

Since we're on the topic of family drama, let's talk about that some more. No matter how laid back and easy going you may be - no matter how chilled you are when planning your wedding - there's one thing that you have no control over. Other people. What you do have control over are your reactions. This can also be very hard to control when someone is making this wedding planning process far more difficult that it can be. A bride of mine named Kathy had her share of family drama to deal with. In a nutshell, her parents were divorced and there were some unresolved issues that were far too important to put aside for their daughters big day (apparently). Dad didn't want to pay for the wedding if Mom showed up with her new boyfriend. On the other hand, Mom said she wasn't coming if her new beau wasn't welcome. Dad said he would not be in the same room as the two of them. Kathy was beside herself. Yes, a pickle indeed. She tried to rationalize with her mother and asked her to leave her boyfriend at home just for the sake of her and the wedding. It wasn't about him anyway. It was her day and it was important to her that both her parents be there. If that meant Mom's boyfriend had to miss out then so be it. Nope. Mom wasn't having it. There was no way she was backing down and her boyfriend was sure as hell coming to that wedding. Both parties held their ground and as it stood, her dad was no longer coming to, or funding the wedding. This issue then trickled into her relationship with her fiancé. She suggested they just elope and leave everyone out all together. Well this royally pissed him off because he was not about to enter a marriage where his wife's family controlled his actions. Fair enough, right? Kathy called me in hysterics and explained the whole situation between sobs and begged for my advice. "What the fuck do I do??"

"Well", I said. "You do nothing. You continue along your merry little way as if this issue doesn't exist and it will all sort itself out. You can't control other people. Focus on yourself and how you're going to deal with this. If he's not funding the wedding then you have to see what you have to work with and plan a wedding within that. If it's only a couple thousand dollars then so be it. If you need to take out a loan because it's that important to you then, again, so be it."

Don't let anyone, blood or not, stand in the way of your happiness. If this is affecting your relationship then that's what you really need to focus on because that's your future. If your mother, father, sister or brother chooses to skip out on your wedding, well that's on them. As long as you're always fair and you always do what you think in your heart is right then you've done your bit. The rest is out of your control.

Kathy did just that. Her and her fiancé enrolled in a few marriage classes to help sort out their issues and learn how to deal with different family situations. They learned valuable lessons like how to take certain values and leave certain values out that they've each learned from their families according to what will work for their new family. They continued to plan the wedding according to what they had to work with and what happened? Her mother came around and said her boyfriend was not coming to the wedding because she didn't want to make the father of the bride uncomfortable. Kathy was THEIR daughter and they both deserved to enjoy the wedding day to the fullest. Everyone was happy and present in the end and what did she have to do? Nothing.

Sometimes you just have to omit yourself from the situation. Dealing with family issues can be tough but it can be far more stressful when you're trying to play ref and rectify everything yourself. People don't listen. Our parents and grandparents come from a different generation. They are far more stubborn and one track minded that we are. My parents, for example, will do the exact opposite of what I request because they just can't feel like they're being told what to do. Ever.

One of my dear friends was dealing with some dramarama as well. Her best man and maid of honour who were married, announced that they were splitting up just weeks before the wedding. One was caught having an affair so naturally they could not stand the sight of each other let alone tolerate a full day playing nice in front of cameras, family and friends. The bride was shattered. She did not need this bullshit so close to the finish line. She pleaded with them to just put their differences aside until the wedding was over. Nope. Which, I suppose is fair enough and I get where they're coming from. They didn't want to look back at pictures of them looking like a happy couple when they despised each other. It was a tough situation for everyone. So this poor girl a week before her wedding had no maid of honour and best man. I gave the same advice to my GF as I gave to my client. Just do nothing. It's your day and at this point there's nothing you can do to change anyone's mind.

The ex-couple was at the wedding with bells on. They were all smiles all night as if nothing ever happened. They didn't take any photos together and barely communicated to each other but they fulfilled their duties and the day went off without a hitch. It was a shame what happened and I'm sure it stung watching their best friends get married while they were going through a divorce but it wasn't the bride and groom's fault. Why should they have to sacrifice their happy day for stupid adults fighting like teenagers? That's why the best man and maid of honour decided to be amicable and play nice for the sake of one day. Once again, the couple didn't have to get involved.

There will be times when shit hits the fan with your family or your friends. The best thing you can do about it is learn how to deal with not dealing with it.

17

Confessions of a Bridesmaid

REAL STORIES FROM FED UP BRIDESMAIDS

I would be honored to pretend to be honored to be in your wedding party.

someecards

Just as I've met many, many brides, I've met even more bridesmaids. Bridesmaids who were so fed up with their bride to be that they were nice enough to completely throw them under the bus and provide me with complaints that I can share with you. Being a bridesmaids means dishing out close to $1000, if not more, during the tenure of the lovely couples engagement. That money is allocated - but not limited to - catering to the bride, events leading up to the big day, gifts, hair, make-up and purchasing God awful dresses. Here are their stories.

"Mary's wedding was a total nightmare from the get go. Right off the top of my head, how about make sure you have food for your girls?! On the morning of her wedding day we woke up ready to indulge in a delicious breakfast only to find nothing. Mary was trying to find a hair salon to do her hair - why the hell wasn't this worked out months ago?! Her sister was off at MAC getting her makeup done - thanks for the heads up - and her mother was putting the finishing touches on the wedding dress. Another item that should have been checked off the list weeks in advance! We ended up having to run around trying to get our makeup and hair done; we got dressed and made it to the ceremony just on time, sweaty, famished and parched. Because everything was so unorganized and last minute we obviously didn't have any food for the photos - nor did we have any time to pick anything up because we were constantly running late - so by the time we got to the reception I was so hungry I contemplated eating my bouquet. Once we saw the sight of food we charged the servers like lions pouncing on gazelles. Moral of the story: Feed your bridesmaids."

Danielle, Bridesmaid to Mary, September 2012

***

"Being in about two dozen bridal parties, you can kind of say I'm an expert at being a bridesmaid. Move over Katherine Heigl because by the end of this year I'll surpass your 27 dresses. Some of these weddings were a delight and some were not so much, to say the least. If I had to single out one it would be Connie's wedding. I didn't make it to the end of the altar because I gracefully pulled out of this wedding. There's Bridezilla and then there's Connie. I just couldn't do it anymore. At the beginning of this journey, Connie was great. She seemed super easy going because she asked us all to pick our own dresses. She claimed she didn't care and just wanted us to be comfortable in whatever style we liked best. As long as they were in the blush/cream/pink colour palette. Easy, right? This was convenient because we all had different schedules and we could just go on our own time at our own pace to chose our dresses. She simply asked that we snap a pic and send it to her for approval before purchasing. I found the perfect dress and send it over. Oops, she said, she didn't want anyone wearing lace. Fine, I continued my search. Next dress, snapped a photo and sent it over. Uh-oh, she said again, it's strapless. Fine. Found myself a nice long simple blush dress with thin straps. Nope - can't be long. Only the maid of honour can be in a long dress. Next, that one's almost white. Then, she didn't

179

like the material. This went on and on. Finally she approved one that was on sale. This redeemed her behaviour as I was saving a ton of money so I made the purchase. When she saw it on she hated it. Was it just me? I asked the other girls how their luck was going and they were dealing with the same bullshit. I think Connie would have been better off just choosing all our dresses and not giving us any choice.

Moving along, we tried to plan her bridal shower which we all had to pay for. After we pretty much purchased and organized everything she wanted full details. We tried to emphasize that it was meant to be a surprise but she wanted to head the planning. All our efforts went out the window because she changed everything. By the time the bachelorette came, which was a trip to Vegas (we had to pay our own way and pitch in for her so she got a free trip out of it) I had tapped out. I had already wasted nearly $500 on a dress I couldn't return and shower items that went to waste. This is where I drew the line. Needless to say, Connie and I are no longer friends."

Denise, bridesmaid to Connie, November 2011

***

"I'm not the skinniest girl. I'm ok with it. My friend Julia was not. She had asked me to be in her bridal party - which was a total honour for about a week. She then sent out an email asking everyone to lose weight! BUT - we weren't allowed to be as skinny as her. Which would have been impossible for all of us anyway because she weighed about 110 lbs soaking

wet. She said she was ordering all the dresses in a size six and we'd basically have no choice but to fit in them. According to her this was great "incentive" to lose weight. I was so insulted. What kind of a friend is that? I saw through my obligation, I barely made it into my dress and through the night. I couldn't eat anything with the fear of exploding out of it but I made it and I haven't spoken to her since."
Angela, Bridesmaid of Julia, June 2013

***

"During my friend Penny's engagement I fell pregnant. This was great news for me but awful news for her. Once I told her I sensed being shut out a bit. I know it was bad timing but it was a surprise to me too and aside from the wedding which I was still more than happy to be a part of, I was so excited about it. We had been trying for a while and I just didn't expect it to happen anytime soon! I thought she would be excited too considering she was my best friend and knowing how much we struggled to conceive. She'd send emails without including me in them and she even organized looking for dresses with everyone without me. I was a bit hurt but gave her the benefit of the doubt and thought that maybe this was her way of being considerate. Maybe she thought I had severe morning sickness and she didn't want to bother me? Nope. Finally after a few more meetings I wasn't a part of, I approached her to see what was going on. I was already replaced and she told me she just didn't want me to ruin her pictures. This clearly created a wedge in our friendship. I tried to keep in touch and make an effort to show I still cared about her wedding but I didn't get the same in return. Not once had she asked me how I was feeling or anything about my pregnancy. When the wedding rolled around I didn't even receive an invite. She had told a mutual friend that since I was in my third trimester that I probably wouldn't have been able to come anyway."

Eva, bridesmaid of anonymous, July 2011

***

"My friend Lisa had the longest engagement ever. For just over 3 years she was the soon to be Mrs. Taylor. I found out quickly that during this time nothing was allowed to go on. It was "HER engagement period". Well, I started dating my now husband a few months before she had started dating hers. Once she was engaged she made a lot of passing jokes that I wasn't allowed to get engaged until after she got married. Surely, she was joking, I thought. I understand if she had a shorter engagement, but just because her beau got down on one knee and gave her a ring before mine did doesn't mean I wasn't allowed to get married in at least 4 years? That's just insane, I thought. Well, my husband proposed about a year in to her engagement and because we don't believe in half a decade engagement periods, we set a date for early in the following year. Which was still over a year before her big day! Mine would come and go and she'd still be enjoying "HER engagement year" Nope. She flipped her lid. She called my husband and blasted him for proposing and demanded I at least wait until after she got married to get married myself. I said no way. She may have wanted an extended engagement but we only needed a few months to plan a simple day with about 60 people. I had no interest in waiting 3 years to get married just so she could have the spotlight. Her's would definitely "out-do" mine anyway so what was the problem? I didn't give a shit about any of that stuff. I told her we'd completely focus on her wedding and I wouldn't overshadow hers, that getting married sooner and starting a family was important to me. That her demanding this from me was a bit selfish. We were all entitled to be happy. I still asked her to be my maid of honour as well. Not only did she decline, she tout suite'd me out of her wedding party."

Giulia, bridesmaid to Lisa, November 2013

***

"I never knew how much of a child my cousin was until she got married. I actually never knew that an adult was capable of acting the way she did leading up to her wedding. We were out looking for dresses and she found one that she fell head over heels in love with. Then she saw the price tag. It was out of her budget. She called her dad who was paying for the dress and asked if he could make an exception. He simply said, "Look I'm already giving you $3000 for your dress. Anything beyond that you'll have to pay for yourself." This to me already sounded beyond generous. The whaling began. She was literally stomping her feet, crying and snotting all over the boutique. I was just dumbfounded. If my eyes bulged anymore they would have fallen out of their sockets. The stylist was not phased at all - clearly she'd witnessed this kind of behaviour before. All I heard was "you are so SELFISH!...You're ruining the HAPPIEST DAY of MY LIFE!...you're an asshole...I HATE YOU!" Click.

I thought maybe that was a one-off tantrum. Maybe when you get engaged, your emotions run wild and you see something you want and you just snap? Maybe, if it was JUST a one-off tantrum. She had a few more similar outbursts over the next few months. Every single time she didn't get her way. Then on the big day we all prayed that it would go off without a hitch. Well, karma's a bitch when you're an ungrateful little brat and on the morning of the wedding there were tornado warnings it was raining so heavily. I thought she was going to pass out from all the screaming and crying. She sounded she was hyperventilating and the vein in the centre of her forehead looked like it was going to burst. A friend of mine calls this the vein of extreme emotion. We get it when we smile or cry. This was on a whole new level of extreme emotion. It was throbbing. The rest of the day went the same way. She was miserable and hated every second of it. To this day she still says that her wedding was completely ruined. Thank God that's over."

Heather, bridesmaid to Stacey, September 2014

***

18

Real Brides Advice

BRIDES THAT SAID COULDA, SHOULDA,
WOULDA...

After the hype is over and the Mr. and Mrs. have settled into their nests, I always like to hear what they would have done differently for their weddings. It's amazing how something can be the be-all-and-end-all of your wedding one day and a complete waste of money (literally) the next.

For Chloe and Mark it was the venue. Chloe was dead set on a venue right smack in the middle of the city with a panoramic view of the city skyline. At the time of planning, Chloe recalls thinking that the extra $60 per person was totally reasonable for the breathtaking view and downtown atmosphere. Now, six months later she looks back at it as a total waste. Although she remembers only good things about their special day and doesn't really regret anything, in hindsight she says should have opted for a more convenient and affordable location. The upside to the venue was the uniqueness of it, the view and the pictures that came out of it. The downsides were that guests had to find and pay for parking, they had to travel halfway across the city after the ceremony, aside from the view there was really nothing special about a room with glass walls so as a result they had to majorly decorate, and the obvious point that it was super expensive. With 180 guests they paid nearly $11,000 for a view! Not only that, but she also had to slash her guest list. 180 may seem like a lot of people, but coming from very large families and both having large social circles, they had to omit a lot of people because the capacity of the room was only 175. She said, "If we could go back, I don't care where we'd have it because at the end of the day it was fun and it would have been just as fun in my parents backyard. One thing I would consider before anything is the size of the room. We couldn't invite a lot of people and now that I look back, I really wish they were there."

***

Andrea and Paul were the opposite. When they look back they wish they had spent more money! Weird, right? They didn't have a wedding coordinator.

When they booked their venue they were told they get an "on-site coordinator" included in their booking. Bonus, they thought. They were referred to me through a friend and met with me reluctantly because they already had a wedding planner (so they thought). We went through a few things and I explained my services. They basically concluded that it was a bit of a waste of money and not something they made room for in their budget. After all, what more could I possibly do for them? Fair enough, I thought, to each their own. I wished them all the best and we parted ways. I didn't hear from them again until a year later when Andrea called me in hysterics. "I don't know if you remember me but we met a while back and I said I didn't need you but now I do! Please help!" After calming her down and finding out that her wedding was just two weeks away, on the busiest weekend of the year, I couldn't help her. I was booked solid. I spoke to some of my fellow wedding planners and they too were either booked up or on holidays. Andrea was stuck and in a panic. I tried to help her get organized as best as I could during that week by sending her checklists and by giving her as much advice as possible but couldn't do much more than that. I spoke to Andrea after the wedding and if she could have a once over, she said she'd have a wedding planner right from the start. That budget she couldn't fit me in at the start ended up inflating by 20% and she had the burden of doing everything herself. If she had hired me, not only would she have saved that extra 20%, but my cost of 18% would have been incorporated into the budget and I would have ended up paying for myself with all the discounts I would have passed along to them from my trusted vendors.

*****

"Oh, I'll just do that later. I've got TONS of time" This was my friend Analisa's signature line when she was preparing for her wedding day. Two months out and there were so many little things to take care of. Favours, centerpieces, decor - all DIY that she thought would be a piece of cake. "Seriously, how long could it possibly take to tie a few ribbons?", she kept saying. All those things added up and at her bachelorette weekend, instead of relaxing by the lake we were DIY'ing. It was a bit of a letdown. I didn't want to say, "I told you so" but while up at the cottage Ana was very apologetic and wished she hadn't procrastinated everything. Her bachelorette was more of a workshop than a party. Now she's 4 months pregnant and literally has her whole nursery ready, her baby bag is packed and ready to go and she's bought everything right down to the diapers and baby wipes. Needless to say, she's learned from her past mistake and will never leave anything to the last minute again.

*****

Marina and Hugh, on the other hand, were perfectly happy with everything. When I asked her nearly a year after they were married to give me some regrets she said, "We don't regret any of our expenditures. In hindsight, we're so happy we had a big wedding. Money well spent!"

This is a perfect example of spending within your means no matter what end of the financial scale you're on. Mare and Hugh had an above average budget compared to a lot of people. They married at an exclusive downtown venue, they had filled the entire room with gorgeous flowers and brought in a customized vinyl dance floor with their logo on it. The head table was completely bling-ed out as were they and their bridal party in designer dresses and suits. But it was customized to them. You shouldn't be comparing your wedding or your budget to other people. It's all relative and everyone is different. These two did what was right for them and in the end had THEIR perfect wedding. It's when people go outside of their comfort zone to impress others that they may regret their purchases because they simply couldn't afford it at the time. Not when they spend a little extra here and there simply because they can.

***

If Adriana and Johnny could go back they'd be a little stricter with their guest list. Although they wanted to please their parents and allow them to invite their friends and coworkers, as a result, their guest list was cut significantly. Adriana found herself tossing up which friends she'd have attend her big day over others. It was a complete pain in the ass. Once you open the flood gates and allow your families to invite a few, those few become a few dozen and when you only have a capacity of 150 people, well, that's a third of your guest list. If that wasn't frustrating enough, on the day of the wedding the couple found themselves doing more introductions with people they've never met before rather than enjoying their wedding day to the fullest. Their words of wisdom? Give your parents a number - a very small number – and stick to it. Yes, it's their day too. But it's more yours and your requests should come first. If you're deadest on allowing your families to have their own guest lists then make sure you choose a venue that can accommodate.

***

19

Tips for the Wedding Day

So, not sure if you've worked this out yet or not, but from the moment you go from being a girlfriend to a fiancée, you change. You become obsessed with things you never knew existed and you basically become a total girl.

There's nothing wrong with wanting to put on a celebration that's magical and most importantly FUN. Along the way the crazy bitch in you may come out here and there but on the wedding day you need to be calm. Don't forget what it's all about. You're getting married! The wedding planning has come to an end and it's time to party. Here's what you need to keep in mind:

The Night Before
1. While hanging out with your girls, throw on a pair of socks and your wedding shoes. This will break

them in so you can wear them as long as possible. Which still won't be until the end of the night so accept that from now.

2. Get your overnight bag ready and appoint someone to remind you to take it.

3. Have a couple drinks and enjoy the last night but don't drink too much. You do not want to be hungover and puffy-eyed on your wedding day.

4. Get all the girls dresses and shoes ready. Hanging dresses make for great photos - you don't want to be scrambling around on the day - you want to have everything ready when the photographer gets there.

5. Get a good night's sleep. It's easy to get caught up in the slumber party of it all because lets be real, when was the last time you had your best friends sleep over? Wrap it up, pick a day to do it again where you won't have a curfew and go to sleep.

The Big Day

6. Wake up on the right side of the bed and wake up early. No one likes a cranky bride. Go for a walk if you can squeeze one it. And take it all in. You're getting married today!

7. Coat your stomach. Have a yummy balanced breakfast with enough protein and more than enough

carbs. The drinking is going to start in a few minutes.

8. CHAMPAGNE! Disclaimer: Make sure #7 is done first.

9. Put your phone away and do not take it out again until the very next day. Who the hell are you texting anyway? If they're not in the room with you then you made some bad choices. Instagram and Facebook will also survive without you for 24 hours. Let the others do the posting. When I see brides posting photos on their wedding day it just says "I'm a loser" to me.

10. By the time you're up and starting to get ready your wedding coordinator should be on site. They're the ones with the emergency kit, timelines, schedules and checklists so you don't need to worry about any of the logistics. Just relax and don't rush. When you rush you get flustered, you sweat, you get pit stains and your chest gets all blotchy. Well, at least that's what happens to me.

11. Pace the drinking. It's going to be a long day.

12. Switch OFF. What's done is done. What's about to happen can't be avoided. Be PRESENT and enjoy every single aspect of your day. It's only about eight hours long if you're lucky. Time won't stop and it will be over before you know it. Everything else on your mind can just go away and be confident that any

issues will sort themselves out or be dealt with by someone else - like your wedding planner. That's why you hired them.

13. Embrace the unexpected. Shit will go wrong. Things will be forgotten. An argument may erupt. You may spill something on yourself and someone will definitely be puking by the end of the night. Anything can happen. It's important to embrace it, have a laugh and continue on with your day. Unless of course it's catastrophic - but it's usually not. Brush it off and get back to the party.

14. Accept the fact that you can't talk to and thank everyone. Receiving lines are great for this. If you say "thanks" to everyone as you greet them then if you don't happen to get to them all night it's not a huge issue. Don't feel obligated to be a host all night. The obligation is to enjoy it to the absolute max.

15. Be a guest at your own wedding. You've done enough work leading up to this day. You also have a job which you've been juggling with the planning. You've played tour guide with your out of town guests and you've hired a wedding planner. Time to kick back and watch the show as well as be emerged in it.

16. Don't forget to eat. I hate when people say "oh I didn't get a chance to eat at my own wedding!" Why

the hell not? Were you serving the food? Were you in the kitchen plating up? Doubtful. No reason not to eat the delicious food that YOU picked because it was so delicious. Park yourself in your chair and eat with your husband for the first time as a Mr. and Mrs. No one wants you doing thank you rounds anyway. Because everyone's eating and I'm sure I don't speak only for myself when I say I hate being interrupted when I'm eating.

17. Don't do the garter and bouquet toss. It's super cheesy. This goes for all other wedding games. They`re off limits.

18. Speeches. Keep them short. No inside jokes. Don't have thirty people get up and talk. Limit it to parents, the best man (this is the only speech people want to hear because it's usually funny) and the couple. I know you may think people will be clutching at napkins because the speeches will pull their heart strings, but they won't. No one cares.

19. Throw on your flats. Your shoes have been seen and they've been photographed. They're probably killing you despite the bucket of ice you had them in on the way to the reception after the photos. Anything from here on in is just torture. Take them off, throw on the flats and allow them to go back to their natural size.

20. DANCE! Do not get off the dance floor. Unless it's to pee. I didn't pee because I didn't want to miss anything. Not the most comfortable. So definitely pee.

21. Steal your husband away for a couple minutes every hour. You'll both be pulled in different directions and you'll find that you're not spending much time together. Which is not a big deal because you're kind of spending the rest of your lives together. BUT you'll never get this moment back. Grab him, pick a corner and just watch. Take it all in. It's pretty fucking magical. They're all here for you.

22. Don't have expectations about the wedding night. You hear everyone saying, "Pfff we were sleeping before we hit the bed we were so exhausted!" And the competitive bitch in you barks, "Well, that's not going to be us because we're wild and so in love so we're definitely doing it in the limo on the way and then again in the room, and then again...ALL NIGHT!" Yeah, don't do that. You might. You might not. It's not a big deal because it IS a long day and you'll be tipsy and exhausted, you may just want to pass out. You have the rest of your lives - starting with the relaxing honeymoon. And it's not bad luck not to get down on your wedding night. You know how I feel about superstitions. They're bullshit.

Conclusion

Just like your wedding engagement period should be, I'm going to keep this short. Your wedding will be an amazingly unforgettable day. You'll laugh and you'll cry – happy tears I hope – and you'll dance the night away. And then it will be over. Don't go out of your way to make it this huge production that will soon be forgotten. There is far more to life than this one special day. Stay grounded, spend within your means, and make sure that everything you're doing, you're doing for you and your spunky hubby. Not for the spectators. If you always keep this mentality, your day will be absolutely perfect and one you'll never regret.

BeLaV Weddings Website

BeLaV wedsite BARCODE for those who would like to inquire about wedding planning.

Instagram

Scan this BARCODE to see BeLaV`s Instagram for #allthingspretty @belavwithlove

Pinterest

Scan this BARCODE to follow us on Pinterest and make sure you head to our PINTEREST FAILS board!

About the Author

Bessy Vazzocchi was born and raised in Toronto, Canada. She currently lives between Toronto and Melbourne with her husband. They are expecting their first baby and this is her first book.

37274590R00124